Evidence-Based Offender Profiling

Offender profiling is an investigative tool used to narrow down the range of potential suspects for a crime by predicting the personality, behavioral, and demographic characteristics that an offender is likely to possess, based upon information collected at the crime scene. While offender profiling has been popularized by TV shows and movies such as *Criminal Minds*, *Silence of the Lambs*, and *Mindhunter*, the real-world impact of offender profiling is largely unknown. This book discusses the history of offender profiling, summarizes research on offender profiling methods, and reviews offender profiling evaluations of accuracy and applied impact.

This book also describes a promising new offender profiling methodology called *evidence-based offender profiling*. This new method relies upon empirical data and scientific methods to develop, evaluate, and replicate offender profiles, thereby increasing offender profiling's accuracy and utility for active police investigations. It uses prior information about statistical regularities between types of offenders and types of offenses to predict the characteristics of offenders in unsolved cases. A discussion of the future of offender profiling research and implications for law enforcement is also included.

This book also explains how practitioners can benefit from the use of empirically tested and validated profiles in their unsolved investigations and how the use, continued research, and evaluation of evidence-based offender profiling can advance the quality, prestige, and utility of the field of offender profiling.

Bryanna Fox is Associate Professor of Criminology at the University of South Florida and studies the psychological and developmental risk factors for criminal behavior, forensic psychology, and evidence-based policing. She previously served as an FBI Special Agent and research fellow in the FBI's Behavioral Science Unit and received an Early Career Award from the American Society of Criminology's Division of Developmental and Life-Course Criminology in 2017. Her research can be found in outlets including *Criminal Justice and Behavior*; *Psychological Bulletin*; *Law and Society Review*; *Social Forces*, *Development and Psychopathology*; and the *Journal of Criminal Justice*.

David P. Farrington, O.B.E., is Emeritus Professor of Psychological Criminology at the Institute of Criminology, Cambridge University. He received the Stockholm Prize in 2013, and he has received the four major awards of the American Society of Criminology.

Andreas Kapardis is Emeritus Professor of Legal Psychology in the Department of Law at the University of Cyprus. He was formerly a faculty member in the School of Law at La Trobe University in Australia and is currently Visiting Professor at the Institute of Criminology, Cambridge University. In recognition of his work, he was elected a Full Member of the European Academy of Sciences and Arts in 2016 and is a Life Member of Clare Hall, Cambridge University. His research and teaching interests lie mainly in criminology, criminal justice, legal psychology, and penology.

Olivia C. Hambly is a social researcher within the Government of the United Kingdom. Olivia received her PhD in 2018 from the International Research Centre for Investigative Psychology at the University of Huddersfield. Her thesis focused on the psychological interpretations of domestic burglary offender styles, patterns, and offender characteristics.

Routledge Studies in Criminal Behaviour

Pathways to Sexual Aggression
Edited by Jean Proulx, Eric Beauregard, Patrick Lussier, and Benoit Leclerc

The Psychology of Crime, Policing and Courts
Edited by Andreas Kapardis and David P. Farrington

The Sexual Murderer
Offender Behaviour and Implications for Practice
Eric Beauregard and Melissa Martineau

Psychological Violence in the Workplace
New Perspectives and Shifting Frameworks
Emily Schindeler, Janet Ransley and Danielle Reynald

Domestic Homicide
Patterns and Dynamics
Marieke Liem and Frans Koenraadt

Intergenerational Continuity of Criminal and Antisocial Behaviour
An International Overview of Studies
Edited by Veroni I. Eichelsheim and Steve G. A. van de Weijer

Evidence-Based Offender Profiling
Bryanna Fox, David P. Farrington, Andreas Kapardis and Olivia C. Hambly

For more information about this series, please visit: www.routledge.com/ Routledge-Studies-in-Criminal-Behaviour/book-series/RSCB

Evidence-Based Offender Profiling

Bryanna Fox, David P. Farrington, Andreas Kapardis and Olivia C. Hambly

R Routledge
Taylor & Francis Group

LONDON AND NEW YORK

First published 2020 by Routledge

2 Park Square, Milton Park, Abingdon, Oxon OX14 4RN

605 Third Avenue, New York, NY 10017

Routledge is an imprint of the Taylor & Francis Group, an informa business

First issued in paperback 2021

Publisher's Note

The publisher has gone to great lengths to ensure the quality of this reprint but points out that some imperfections in the original copies may be apparent.

British Library Cataloguing-in-Publication Data
A catalogue record for this book is available from the British Library

Library of Congress Cataloging-in-Publication Data
A catalog record for this book has been requested

ISBN: 978-0-367-35015-4 (hbk)
ISBN: 978-1-03-217412-9 (pbk)
DOI: 10.4324/9780429329340

Typeset in Times New Roman
by Apex CoVantage, LLC

Contents

Acknowledgements

This book is based on papers delivered at an international conference on "Enhancing police criminal investigations with evidence-based offender profiling" at the University of Cyprus on October 16, 2018. This conference was sponsored by the Global College of Cyprus, and we are very grateful to them for their funding.

Foreword

The rise of evidence-based policing over the past half-century has taken many forms (Sherman, 2013). None of them is more compelling than the idea that criminology can contribute to catching criminals and even convicting them. The promise of this very welcome new book, *Evidence-Based Offender Profiling*, is to do just that.

Since 2008, the University of Cambridge has offered the largest postgraduate course on evidence-based policing in the world. The Institute of Criminology's part-time master's degree for police leaders and analysts currently enrols about 150 students per year, many of whom go on to lead large police agencies. In the United Kingdom, more than 1 in 10 of the current chief officers (some 233 Chief Constables, deputy constables, and assistant chief constables) are already graduates of the Cambridge course. Police executives from Canada, Australia, Denmark, New Zealand, and Sweden join their UK colleagues to study the latest research findings that can improve police effectiveness under the rule of law. They also contribute their own research by master's theses to such global publications as the *Cambridge Journal of Evidence-Based Policing*.

It is in that context that the material in this book has been tested and triumphed. With most of our students under relentless pressure to raise their agency's clearance rates, the prospect of doubling or tripling those rates seems almost impossible. Yet with a growing body of experimental evidence proving that such gains are possible, our students have seized on the idea of offense–offender profiling as a framework for gathering and digitizing new kinds of data. The articles that precede this book have been the subject of our students' intense interest. Several have gone on to produce research extending these findings, exploring with large data sets the questions of consistency of MOs and the limited number of suspects who share similar modus operandi.

There will, of course, always be differences across cultures and communities in the kinds of crimes that new offenders are recruited – or independently decide – to commit. Burglary rates have dropped in many countries for reasons that are not entirely clear, while frauds appear to have increased with a changing criminal opportunity structure. What one offender may do over many years may be something other offenders do only once before desisting or moving on to more lucrative crimes.

None of these considerations, however, detract in any way from the value of the framework presented in this book. Whatever the patterns of crime faced by any local police establishment, there will be opportunities to use evidence-based offender profiling. The basic logic of comprehensive and systematic analysis of all crimes of a certain category is the polar opposite of what has often been called "offender profiling", but which I would call a "speculation-based" method of looking for suspects for any given crime. This polarity leads us to a rigorous comparison of the people linked to solved crimes and unsolved crimes committed with the same MO. This radically empirical approach requires no speculation. Rather, it requires perspiration and correlation to generate a digital process of elimination.

In the growing digital infrastructure for criminal justice, many more investigators will be able to check whether a suspect was in prison on the date of an offense. Artificial intelligence might even do it for them, producing a list of suspects who can be eliminated, and why – despite their having a history of a similar MO. The upshot will be even greater value for the generation of digital profiles of offender behavior in cases for which they were detected.

Who should read this book? It is a "must-read" for any police professional who is committed to raising the clearance rate for any given offense category. It may be an inspiring read for young people considering careers as investigators. It may be an excellent investment for anyone managing police budgets, so they can judge the potential value of creating "digital shoe leather" of the kind this book describes.

As for criminology, the book is a welcome reminder that criminology is as essential to reducing crime as biochemistry is to reducing illness. Criminology is many things to many people. As this book shows, criminology is certainly an intellectual home for evidence-based policing.

Lawrence W. Sherman
Editor-in-Chief, *Cambridge Journal of Evidence-based Policing*
Cambridge, UK

Reference

Sherman, Lawrence W. (2013). The rise of evidence-based policing: Targeting, testing, and tracking. *Crime and Justice 42*, 377–451.

1 Introduction to *Evidence-Based Offender Profiling*

Introduction

Offender profiling is arguably one of the most popular and salient topics in the field of criminology. We have all seen offender profiling portrayed on hit TV shows and films such as *Criminal Minds*, *The Silence of the Lambs*, *Cracker*, and *Mindhunter*, and heard the legendary tales of "profilers" catching elusive serial killers and other horrific offenders. In each case, profilers are depicted as having psychic-like talents used to predict features of an unknown offender based upon behaviors at the crime scene alone. So, how accurate is this portrayal?

Consider the case of the Mad Bomber, who terrorized New York City in the 1940s to 1950s until police, at their wits' end, asked psychiatrist James Brussel to develop a "profile" to help them catch the responsible offender. As the story goes, Brussel reviewed the files and then provided police an incredibly detailed description of the bomber: a middle-aged man of Eastern European descent living alone in Connecticut; a disgruntled former employee of Con Edison, the city's utility company. Before he left the police station, Brussel told the detectives, "When you catch him, and I have no doubt you will, he'll be wearing a double-breasted suit. And it will be buttoned".

A month later, George Metesky, an unmarried man of Lithuanian descent living in Waterbury, Connecticut, who was previously employed by Con Edison until a dispute in 1931, was arrested by police as the mastermind behind the New York City bombings. When police came to the door, Metesky was in his pajamas and went upstairs to change. When he came back downstairs, he was wearing a double-breasted suit, fully buttoned, just as Brussel predicted.

Stories like these leave us thinking that profilers are a godsend to police work and routinely solve the cases that they work on. However, many experts in the fields of psychology, criminology, and law enforcement have raised serious concerns about the practice, particularly in light of research which suggests that offender profiles are no more accurate than a coin toss. This has led many experts to call offender profiling "less than useless", a total "waste of police time", and other terms that indicate a strong skepticism towards the practice.

So just how accurate are profilers at solving crimes? This important question, first raised in 1976 by former *Psychology Today* Editor Colin Campbell, is critical to determining if profiling is as beneficial as pop culture would lead us to believe. Or, as Colin Campbell wondered, are profilers any better at predicting behavior than a bartender?

This book aims to address this important question, and outlines the development and results from a new approach to offender profiling called evidence-based offender profiling (EBOP). In the chapters that follow, we describe the need for data, statistics, and evidence in the offender profiling field; the EBOP approach and philosophy; and results from empirical studies and evaluations of EBOP. Before that, we provide some background information on the field of offender profiling, its origins, assessments of its accuracy and utility, and the existing approaches to offender profile development. We then describe the state of the offender profiling field and how EBOP can be used to improve the validity and utility of profiles developed and applied in active police investigations around the globe.

Reference

Campbell, C. (1976). Portrait of a mass killer. *Psychology Today*, *9*, 110–119.

2 Development of offender profiling

Introduction

The work of law enforcement around the world is becoming more challenging as criminals are becoming more adept. This emphasizes the need for more sophisticated criminal investigation methods, such as computerized offender profiling. Although clearance rates for different crimes will vary, generally speaking, offenders are caught by police for one of the following reasons: they admit to the crime; police receive a credible tip or have a valid eyewitness; the offender is arrested in the act; there is CCTV footage of the offender at the crime scene; there is forensic evidence such as fingerprints, footprints, or DNA at the crime scene that can be linked to them; or, finally, because the police link multiple crimes to a single known offender. When none of these options are available, investigators are left with very little to generate leads or help solve the case. In those cases, police are left with few opportunities to identify a suspect while new cases come piling in, leaving many crimes to remain unsolved.

Consequently, law enforcement and academics have strived to develop new methods and tools to help identify suspects in cases, based upon behavioral evidence consistently available at crime scenes. One such method is offender profiling. Although different definitions of offender profiling exist, generally speaking, offender profiling is a technique used to identify key personality, behavioral, and demographic characteristics of an offender based on an analysis of the crimes that he or she has committed (Douglas, Ressler, Burgess, & Hartman, 1986). Behavioral data evident in a crime is used to assist a police investigation by seeking to infer attributes of probable offenders, thus narrowing the police search for suspects (Kocsis, 2006; Crighton, 2010).

Many law enforcement agencies across the world already request profiling services on difficult cases, from a Federal Bureau of Investigation (FBI) profiler, a trained law enforcement agent, a profiler in private practice, or an academic consultant trained in psychology, profiling, or behavioral analysis (Kocsis, Hayes, & Irwin, 2002; Trager & Brewster, 2001). While profiling may be used to prioritize and focus police investigations of offenders, a profile does not constitute trial evidence or justify an arrest of an offender; probable cause is still needed to legally arrest a suspect in any given case (*State v. Stevens*, 2001).

Offender profiling has been popularized by films such as *Silence of the Lambs*, television series such as *Cracker* and *Criminal Minds*, books such as *The Real Cracker* by Stephen Cook (2001), *The Jigsaw Man* and *Picking Up the Pieces* by Paul Britton (1998, 2001), and other books by ex-FBI profilers such as John Douglas, Roy Hazelwood, and Robert Ressler on their experiences of helping law enforcement to catch serial killers (see, e.g., Douglas & Olshaker, 1995, 1999, 2000; Hazelwood & Michaud, 2001; Ressler & Schachtman, 1992). To date, hundreds of academic books and journal articles on offender profiling have been published (Fox & Farrington, 2018; see also Alison & Rainbow, 2011; Bartol & Bartol, 2012; Canter & Youngs, 2009; Hicks & Sales, 2006; Turvey, 2011). However, despite the amount of attention, interest, and applied use of offender profiling, it remains unclear where the field currently stands from a scientific standpoint (Fox & Farrington, 2012). While recent research indicates that there have been significant improvements in the scientific rigour of the research conducted, few studies have used a strong empirical approach to develop new profiles, and even fewer have evaluated the usefulness of offender profiling to criminal investigations (Fox & Farrington, 2018; Kocsis, 2003, 2004).

Indeed, scholars and law enforcement have warned about the danger of "overselling" offender profiling by exaggerating its importance and ignoring the fact that the history of offender profiling includes failures (Farrington & Lambert, 2000, p. 236). To illustrate, a early review of the use of offender profiling by Copson (1995) examined 184 cases by police forces in Britain and found that it helped to solve the case only 14% of the time, and helped identify the offender in only 3% of the cases. However, as will be seen in this chapter, offender profiling researchers can now claim greater usefulness of their work to police investigations, but offender profiling is not a panacea. The question of whether offender profiling today is better than "bartenders" at predicting characteristics of offenders has been addressed by Fox and Farrington (2018), and is also discussed in other chapters in this book.

Offender profiling terms and approaches

As stated, there is no single definition or consistent term for "offender profiling" used across the field.[1] However, all definitions agree that the ultimate goal of offender profiling is to establish links between specific types of crimes committed and the characteristics of offenders who have commit those types of crimes. How this goal is accomplished differs greatly across different profiling approaches. For example, Hazelwood and Douglas (1980, p. 22) defined the FBI's approach to offender profiling as

> An educated attempt to provide investigative agencies with specific information as to the type of individual who committed a certain crime. . . . A profile is based on the characteristic patterns or factors of uniqueness that distinguish certain individuals from the general population.

This is an example of a *clinical approach* to offender profiling, as the FBI used interviews with offenders and subjective interpretation of crime scenes (and little scientific methodology) to develop their profiles. There are also *statistical approaches* to offender profiling that rely on data, analysis, and replicable methods to develop profiles. These approaches have substantial differences in terms of the background, methodology, results, and applications of the profiles (Fox & Farrington, 2018). However, there appears to be little awareness of these differences among members of the general public, and in some cases, just the name of the profiling approach has a notable impact on the perceptions of the validity and legitimacy of the profiles. Specifically, Torres, Boccanccini, and Miller (2006) surveyed perceptions of the scientific basis of profiling by different mental health professionals. They found that changing the term from "profiling" to "criminal investigative analysis" (while their definitions remained the same) correlated with an increase in perceived validity among the respondents. Therefore, clearly defining and outlining the strengths and weaknesses of each approach is highly beneficial for academics, practitioners, and the general public (Kocsis, 2013; Kocsis & Palermo, 2015; Kocsis, Middledorp, & Karpin, 2008). The two major approaches to offender profiling are described in detail next.

Clinical approaches

In the clinical approach to offender profiling, profiles are developed on a case-by-case basis by a profiler (e.g., a forensic psychiatrist or law enforcement profiler) who has considerable training, experience, and practice in the field, but with no clear methodology described (e.g., Holmes & Holmes, 1996; Snook, Cullen, Bennell, Taylor, & Gendreau, 2008). Many clinical profiles are developed using "experience, intuition, and educated guesswork" (Geberth, 1990, p. 492; Pinizzotto, 1984) and are not based on quantitative data and statistical methods (Fox & Farrington, 2015; Kocsis & Cooksey, 2002). However, clinical profiling also allows for a more customized and informed profile to be developed, which is preferred by some investigators and profilers. While there are many examples of clinical profiles and their applications, this chapter focuses on three famous case studies and on the FBI's clinical approach to profiling. It highlights the benefits and limitations of an offender profile constructed on the basis of subjective clinical work.

Jack the Ripper

In the autumn of 1888 in London, the killer who came to be known as Jack the Ripper murdered at least five female prostitutes, all within a mile of each other, by cutting their throats and mutilating their bodies (see Sugden, 1995). Such brutal crimes were unlike almost anything else seen by 19th century Britons, and the fact that the killer was able to continue his murderous spree for over two months was shocking and fear-inducing for residents. To better understand the case, police consulted Dr. Thomas Bond, a surgeon, to shed light on the nature and skill required in the mutilation and organ removals by the killer.

After reviewing the crime scene photos and autopsy results, Bond believed that these murders were all committed by the same offender. In fact, Bond opined that the killer was a man suffering from occasional attacks of homicidal and erotic mania (Sugden, 1995) and that, despite the extensive knife wounds, the killer had no formal medical training or knowledge of anatomy, given the lack of precision in the cuts. Bond also coined the term "signature" to refer to the similar behaviors seen across offenses but not required to commit the crimes. In the case of Jack's murders, Bond believed that the extensive mutilation, and in some cases, removal of internal organs, was his signature.

Despite this innovative new approach to investigating serial offenders, and the more than 2,000 people interviewed, 300 people investigated (including butchers and high-profile suspects), and 80 people detained, the killer was never caught. This case became one of England's most infamous unsolved mysteries, feeding an industry of films, TV series, and books for decades to come.

The Yorkshire Ripper, Peter Sutcliffe

The importance of police being able to accurately link crimes to a single offender is well exemplified in the case of the "Yorkshire Ripper" in England. Between 1975 and 1980, at least 13 people were killed in Yorkshire cities by an offender who police did not identify until well into the horrible crime spree (Farrington & Lambert, 2000). Peter Sutcliffe was finally arrested for these offenses in 1981 after police found him in a car with false number plates, with a prostitute, and resembling the photofit of the Yorkshire Ripper suspect. He was later convicted of 13 murders and seven attempted murders.

Many people criticized the failure to link the crimes sooner, particularly as more than half of the females were known prostitutes, the offender generally attacked his victims from behind with a hammer, and he left the bodies in degrading positions (Farrington & Lambert, 2000). This failure was even more shocking considering that Sutcliffe was convicted in 1969 for attempting to assault a prostitute with a hammer in Bradford, he was interviewed by the police nine times between 1977 and 1980, and police received an anonymous letter naming Sutcliffe as the killer of his second victim in 1975 (Farrington & Lambert, 2000).

Unfortunately, based on a hoax tape recording that was sent to the police, they believed that the offender came from the North East of England and had a "Geordie" accent. Sutcliffe has a Yorkshire accent. While there was misinformation and inaccurate leads provided in the case, if the police had been able to link these murders sooner, a clearer profile of the suspect would have been developed, and it is very likely that some lives would have been saved.

The Mad Bomber, George Metesky

For 16 years in the 1940s and 1950s, New York City was terrorized by 33 self-made bombs planted in public places by an offender who came to be known as the "Mad Bomber". After years of investigations led to dead ends, the New York Police Department contacted psychiatrist James Brussel to help to develop a profile of the characteristics that this type of offender would most likely possess, based upon the available investigative information.

After reviewing the case files, Brussel's profile was as follows: a middle-aged foreign-born man, likely Roman Catholic and of Eastern European decent, who lived in Connecticut either alone or with a sibling, had mechanical skills and was likely to be a disgruntled former employee of the city's utility company, Con Edison (Brussel, 1968). Perhaps most infamously, Brussel also predicted that the "Mad Bomber" was a smart dresser, and when police caught him, he would likely be "wearing a double-breasted suit. And it will be buttoned" (Brussel, 1968).

Soon after, Con Edison searched their internal records for disgruntled employees matching Brussel's profile and came across the file of George Metesky, an unmarried Lithuanian immigrant living in Waterbury, Connecticut, previously employed by Con Edison until he was fired after a work accident in 1931, which left him without a pension (Brussel, 1968). When police went to Metesky's house late in the evening on January 21, 1957, he was initially wearing his pajamas, but after changing, he came back wearing a double-breasted suit, fully buttoned, just as Brussel had predicted. In fact, Metesky fit many other elements of Brussel's profile, which led many to believe that offender profiling was a failproof strategy that police could use to help to identify suspects in unsolved cases. However, while this example is impressive, it is important not to overlook the fact that the clinical approach is largely subjective and falls short of the scientific reliability required in the critical environment of major crime investigations (Rainbow, 2011a, p. 1).

FBI's criminal investigative analysis

In the 1970s, Special Agent Howard Teten and his colleagues in the FBI's Behavioral Science Unit (BSU) at the FBI Academy in Quantico developed a new approach to offender profiling, called criminal investigative analysis (CIA). While clinical in nature, this approach represented an improvement on the earlier clinical approaches which did not rely on research or data analysis in forming the offender profiles. Specifically, members of the BSU aimed to better understand the crimes, motivations, personalities, and behaviors of serial offenders using interviews with 36 of the most infamous apprehended serial killers and murderers of their time, such as Charles Manson, Ed Gein, John Wayne Gacy, Ted Bundy, and others (Hazelwood & Douglas, 1980).

In addition to these qualitative interviews, the agents' collective investigative experience, and some basic data on crime scene and offender features, the agents began to notice that there were patterns in the way that certain crimes were committed, and in the traits, backgrounds, and motivations of the offenders who committed them (see Hazelwood & Burgess, 1987; Hazelwood & Douglas, 1980; Ressler, Burgess, & Douglas, 1988). This led the BSU agents to propose a new offender profiling technique that could be used by police to generate or narrow down the range of possible suspects by predicting a combination of characteristics that an offender was likely to possess based on elements of the crime scene alone. These profiles were developed through a deductive process in which crime scenes were studied in detail to propose specific and customized profiles applicable only to that case and that offender (Holmes & Holmes, 1996). They included information about the offender's personality, age, race, gender, religion, marital status, and other social and behavioral factors.

According to this new approach to offender profiling, all serial murderers, rapists, and arsonists could be classified into "organized" or "disorganized" sub-types (Hazelwood & Douglas, 1980; Hazelwood & Burgess, 1987). Organized crimes are carefully planned and conducted in a methodical manner with any known evidence of the offense destroyed or concealed to prevent detection (Kocsis, Irwin, & Hayes, 1998). Organized offenders take control at the crime scene and are expected to be intelligent (but a likely under-achiever), to have good interpersonal skills, to be sexually competent, to be living with a partner and appearing "normal but harbouring an antisocial or psychopathic personality, carefully follow media accounts of his murders" and may well return to the scene of the crime (Ainsworth, 2001, p. 101). These offenders are typically not known to police, and they go to extraordinary lengths to cover their tracks and avoid being caught, making it very difficult for law enforcement to solve these cases.

By contrast, a disorganized offender is a totally disorganized individual in terms of their criminal activity, as well as their appearance, lifestyle, and psychological state (Holmes & Holmes, 2002). Disorganized offenses are poorly planned or even impetuous, and the victims tend to be chosen at random. These offenses are often committed by inexperienced and reckless offenders near their homes, with little effort made to conceal the crime, often leaving a frenzied and chaotic crime scene typically with evidence left behind (Hazelwood & Douglas, 1980).

Based upon these profiles, profilers are able to advise police on other issues such as investigative techniques to identify suspects and how to question the suspects when they are arrested. For instance, CIA advises that organized offenders should be confronted directly, while a disorganized offender will be more likely to respond to police questioning if the interrogator empathizes with him, establishing a positive personal relationship (Holmes & Holmes, 2002).

That said, the FBI's organized and disorganized profiles and CIA approach have come under scrutiny in recent years, as they were created using "experience, intuition, and educated guesswork" (Geberth, 1990, p. 492; Pinizzotto, 1984) rather than being based on quantitative data and statistical methods (Fox & Farrington, 2012, 2018; Kocsis & Cooksey, 2002). Moreover, the research used to develop the CIA approach was based on a small and biased sample and did not rely on advanced statistical analysis, and many profilers using the same crime scene analysis data would often produce different profiles (Fox & Farrington, 2018).

However, the criticisms levelled against the CIA method must also be weighed against its contribution in occasionally bringing to justice criminals who terrorize communities and would otherwise remain uncaught. Finally, we should not forget that profiling is but one tool available to police investigators and is generally used as an option of last resort (Stevens, 1997, p. 77). That said, predictions based upon statistically generated and methodologically rigorous research tend to be more accurate than clinical predictions (Farrington & Lambert, 2000). There-fore, statistical approaches to offender profiling are discussed next.

Statistical approaches

More recently, efforts have been made to develop and utilize profiles using statistical techniques (e.g., smallest space analysis [SSA]) to more effec-tively analyze offense, offender, victim, and situational characteristics; empirically based classifications; and linkages between them (Howitt, 2002). While this approach is relatively young (first developed in the 1990s by David Canter in response to the FBI's clinical CIA approach), a variety of methods and sub-fields of statistical profiling have been proposed. The following is a brief overview of the most popular statistical approaches to offender profiling.

Investigative psychology

Investigative psychology (IP) is a statistical approach to profiling offenders which has, largely under the aegis of David Canter, evolved to a specialized discipline within the broader field of criminology and psychology (Canter, 2011; Canter & Youngs, 2003, 2009). IP researchers aim to identify statisti-cal patterns in a broad range of criminal behaviors, which can be used to help investigators to better understand and predict suspects in particular cases (Canter, 1995a). As an example, Canter (1995b) examined the sta-tistical relationship between characteristics of rape offenses (e.g., whether the offender bound up the victim or forced the victim to masturbate him) and the responsible offenders' characteristics, such as previous convictions for indecent exposure or indecent assault (see also Canter & Kirby, 1995). Others have used the IP approach to identify unique sub-types of arson-ists (Canter & Fritzon, 1998), property offenders (Canter & Alison, 2000), armed robbers (Alison, Rockett, Deprez, & Watts, 2000), and the relation-ship between murder crime scenes and the characteristics of responsible offenders (Salfati & Canter, 1999).

To do this, IP researchers typically use multidimensional scaling (MDS), which is a statistical analysis that evaluates latent themes in mul-tivariate data by calculating the inter-relationships between variables and presenting the results in a multidimensional similarity matrix (Davis, 2009; Takane, Young, & De Leeuw, 1977). In MDS, items that are more similar and that more commonly co-occur in the data are plotted closer together in the multidimensional output (Coxon, 1982). One version of MDS that has been popularized in the criminological and psychological fields is SSA, which produces a solution of the smallest dimensionality amongst all variables after a correlation matrix is transformed into a three-dimensional rank-ordered similarity matrix presented in the form of spatial output (Guttman, 1954).

To determine the number and nature of sub-types in the data, MDS plots are visually examined and interpreted based upon the proximity of variable clusters co-occurring in the output map (Alison & Stein, 2001; Canter, Bennell, Alison, & Reddy, 2003; Canter & Heritage, 1990; Guttman, 1954). No quantitative data are provided to indicate the probability of each item occurring in each resultant sub-type. This is a limitation of the MDS approach, among other limitations that have sparked a debate on MDS in recent years (see Davis, 2009; Goodwill, Alison, & Beech, 2009; Sturidsson et al., 2006, 2009).

Concerning criticism of the broader IP approach, Kocsis (2006) believes that there has not been any independently conducted, empirically robust, and scientifically peer-reviewed study that demonstrates that a sample of suitably qualified experts in IP can construct an accurate criminal profile of the characteristics of an unknown offender any better than individuals employing some other rivalling method of profiling. It would appear that the controversy between investigative psychologists and Kocsis is attributable to their different preferred conceptualizations of offender profiling and, consequently, the different methodologies they use. Of course, from a police investigator's point of view, the use of the statistical approach would not stop a police investigator from also utilizing an offender profile constructed by a clinician.

Crime linkage analysis

As described in the case of the Yorkshire Ripper, it is highly beneficial for police to be able to link cases to the same offender with high degree of accuracy (Fox & Farrington, 2016). Crime linkage analysis (CLA), first developed by Bennell and Canter (2002), uses statistical analysis to link crimes to a single offender on the basis of commonalities seen across crime scene behaviors. CLA generally uses receiver operating characteristic (ROC) analysis to evaluate the level of behavioral similarity across multiple offenses and determine the likelihood of cases being committed by the same offender (Bennell, Mugford, Ellingwood, & Woodhams, 2014). Area under the ROC curve (AUC) analysis is used to assess the accuracy of the decision to link crimes to a serial offender (Bennell et al., 2014; Steadman et al., 2000). Given the statistical sophistication of CLA, this approach has been a rapidly growing area in the offender profiling field.

For instance, Santtila et al. (2008) reported 62.9% classification accuracy when linking 116 homicides to 23 individual offenders based entirely upon behaviors at the crime scenes, indicating the potential usefulness of CLA to investigators. Bennell et al. (2014) evaluated all CLA research published between 2002 and 2013 and found that burglary and sexual assault were the most common crime types in the CLA studies, although accuracy values were the highest for homicide followed by sexual assault, arson, burglary, and then robbery and car theft.

Finally, the meta-analysis of case linkage analysis research by Fox and Farrington (2018) concluded that this area is statistically sophisticated and "has yielded moderate to strong accuracy rates for linking crimes to a single offender" (p. 1247).

Geographic profiling

The geographic examination of crime has existed since the early 1970s (Reppetto, 1974). Geographic profilers, whether drawing on geography or environmental psychology, analyze crime locations to identify a specific area that may be linked to the offender (Rossmo, 2000). For instance, it is widely accepted that most offenders, including serial killers, do not travel very far from their places of residence to commit their crimes (Canter, 1995a; Goodwin & Canter, 1997; Kapardis, 1989). By analyzing crime locations, patterns, and temporal trends, often through the use of mathematical algorithms in computer programs such as Geographical Information Systems (GIS), information about the geographic profiles of offenders can be developed and provide investigators with very useful information about where potential suspects are located.

Consequently, the goal of geographical profiling is the identification and prediction of spatial movements of a single serial offender using statistical analyses, ideally to offer investigators probability estimates regarding where a suspect's residence, work, or future offenses might be located (Rossmo, 2000; Canter, 2003). To do this, many use a computer program known as Criminal Geographic Targeting, developed by Rossmo (1995), to analyze the spatial characteristics of (presumably linked) crimes to produce a topographic map, and then to assign probabilities to different locations where the suspect may be residing, have his base for offending, and/or may offend in the future. Therefore, geographic profiles can be used, often in combination with an offender profile, to provide investigators with a more clear and accurate picture of potential suspects (Rossmo, 1997, 2000).

Geographic profiling has also helped to better understand the hunting process of predatory offenders, such as serial killers. For instance, this research suggests that these offenders have two stages to their "hunting": (1) the search for a suitable victim and (2) the method of attack (Rossmo, 1997). In short, geographic profiles can be used to help police decide where investigative resources should be deployed to have the highest statistical likelihood of identifying the offender or preventing the offense and for police to be more effective and efficient in their work.

Offender profiling: a profession

Today, offender profiling has moved from the early CIA to a more evidence-based approach and into mainstream forensic psychological research. Furthermore, offender profiling in the United Kingdom has become a recognized profession, including the development of the Behavioral Investigative Adviser (BIA) position (Rainbow, 2011a, p. 1). The term BIA has replaced "offender profiler", and the professional and ethical standards of BIAs are regulated at a national level by the Association of Chief Police Officers (ACPO). For full-time BIAs employed within the National Crime Agency, there is a BIA roadmap for professional development (Rainbow, 2011b). For instance, a BIA is tasked with providing investigating officers with "an additional perspective and decision support through a serious crime investigation; an additional 'tool in the box' rather than any magical panacea" (Rainbow & Gregory, 2011, p. 20). Notably, the work of BIAs is greatly assisted by the existence of electronic databases such as the Violent and Sex Offender Register (VISOR) in the UK (akin to the Violent Criminal Apprehension Program, or ViCAP, in the US), which contain data on offender and offense characteristics (Kocsis, 2015). These data-driven approaches are the future of the offender profiling field, and the coming chapters further describe the benefits of statistical and scientific approaches in the field of offender profiling.

Conclusion

Research on offender profiling over the past four decades shows that police, in investigating crime, are more efficient and effective when they utilize and contribute to more statistical and evidence-based offender profiling techniques. As long as researchers are prepared to tackle the challenges presented by crime and criminals constructively and in the field, progress is inevitable, and the development of offender profiling shows this.

Note

1 Fox and Farrington (2018) utilized the following terms for offender profiling in their systematic review and meta-analysis: offender profiling, criminal profiling, psychological profiling, criminal personality profiling, personality profiling, criminal investigative analysis, investigative psychology, behavioral profiling, behavioral evidence analysis, geographic profiling, linkage analysis, crime linkage, crime linkage analysis, crime scene analysis, behavioral linkage, behavior linkage, crime behavior consistency, and behavioral consistency analysis.

References

Ainsworth, P. B. (2001). *Offender profiling and crime analysis*. Cullompton: Willan.

Alison, L. J., & Rainbow, L. (Eds.). (2011). *Professionalizing offender profiling: Forensic and investigative psychology in practice*. New York, NY: Taylor & Francis.

Alison, L. J., Rockett, W., Deprez, S., & Watts, S. (2000). Bandits, cowboys and Robin's men: The facets of armed robbery. In D. Canter & L. Alison (Eds.), *Profiling property crimes* (pp. 75–106). Dartmouth: Ashgate Publishing.

Alison, L. J., & Stein, K. L. (2001). Vicious circles: Accounts of stranger sexual assault reflect abusive variants of conventional interactions. *The Journal of Forensic Psychiatry, 12*(3), 515–538.

Bartol, C. R., & Bartol, A. M. (2012). *Criminal and behavioral profiling*. Thousand Oaks, CA: Sage.

Bennell, C., & Canter, D. V. (2002). Linking commercial burglaries by modus operandi: Tests using regression and ROC analysis. *Science & Justice, 42*(3), 153–164.

Bennell, C., Mugford, R., Ellingwood, H., & Woodhams, J. (2014). Linking crimes using behavioural clues: Current levels of linking accuracy and strategies for moving forward. *Journal of Investigative Psychology and Offender Profiling, 11*, 29–56.

Britton, P. (1998). *The jigsaw man*. London: Corgi Books.

Britton, P. (2001). *Picking up the pieces*. London: Corgi Books.

Brussel, J. A. (1968). *Casebook of a crime psychiatrist*. New York, NY: Simon & Schuster.

Canter, D. V. (1995a). *Criminal shadows: Inside the mind of the serial killer*. London: Harper Collins.

Canter, D. V. (1995b). Psychology of offender profiling. In R. Bull & D. Carson (Eds.), *Handbook of psychology in legal contexts* (pp. 343–355). Chichester: John Wiley & Sons.

Canter, D. V. (2003). *Mapping murder: The secrets of geographical profiling*. London: Virgin Books.

Canter, D. V. (2011). Resolving the offender "profiling equations" and the emergence of an investigative psychology. *Current Directions in Psychological Science, 20*, 5–10.

Canter, D. V., & Alison, L. J. (2000). *Profiling property crimes* (Vol. 4). Aldershot: Ashgate Publishing.

Canter, D. V., Bennell, C., Alison, L. J., & Reddy, S. (2003). Differentiating sex offenses: A behaviourally based classification of stranger rapes. *Behavioral Sciences and the Law, 21*, 157–174.

Canter, D. V., & Fritzon, K. (1998). Differentiating arsonists: A model of firesetting actions and characteristics. *Journal of Criminal and Legal Psychology, 3*, 73–96.

Canter, D., & Heritage, R. (1990). A multivariate model of sexual offence behaviour: Developments in "offender profiling". I. *The Journal of Forensic Psychiatry, 1*(2), 185–212.

Canter, D. V., & Kirby, S. (1995). Prior convictions of child molesters. *Science and Justice, 35,* 73–78.

Canter, D. V., & Youngs, D. (2003). Beyond "offender profiling": The need for an investigative psychology. In D. Carson & R. Bull (Eds.), *Handbook of psychology in legal contexts* (2nd ed., pp. 171–205). Chichester: John Wiley & Sons.

Canter, D. V., & Youngs, D. (2009). *Investigative psychology: Offender profiling and the analysis of criminal action.* Chichester: John Wiley & Sons.

Cook, S. (2001). *The real cracker: Investigating the criminal mind.* London: Channel 4 Books.

Copson, G. (1995). *Coals to Newcastle? Police use of offender profiling.* London: Home Office.

Coxon, A. P. M. (1982). *The user's guide to multi-dimensional scaling with special reference to the MDS (X) library of computer programs.* London: Heinemann Educational.

Crighton, D. A. (2010). Offender profiling. In G. J. Towl & D. Crighton (Eds.), *Forensic psychology* (pp. 148–159). Chichester, West Sussex: BPS Blackwell.

Davis, M. R. (2009). In defence of multidimensional scaling for the analysis of sexual offence behaviour: Cautionary notes regarding analysis and interpretation. *Psychology, Crime & Law, 15*(6), 507–515.

Douglas, J. E., & Olshaker, M. (1995). *Mindhunter: Inside the FBI's elite serial crime unit.* New York, NY: Simon & Schuster.

Douglas, J. E., & Olshaker, M. (1999). *The anatomy of motive.* New York, NY: Pocket Books.

Douglas, J. E., & Olshaker, M. (2000). *The cases that haunt us.* New York, NY: Scribner.

Douglas, J. E., Ressler, R. K., Burgess, A. W., & Hartman, C. R. (1986). Criminal profiling from crime scene analysis. *Behavioral Sciences & the Law, 4*(4), 401–421.

Farrington, D. P., & Lambert, S. (2000). Statistical approaches to offender profiling. In D. V. Canter & L. J. Alison (Eds.), *Profiling property crimes* (pp. 233–274). Aldershot: Ashgate Publishing.

Fox, B., & Farrington, D. P. (2012). Creating burglary profiles using latent class analysis: A new approach to offender profiling. *Criminal Justice and Behavior, 39,* 1582–1611.

Fox, B., & Farrington, D. P. (2015). An experimental evaluation of the utility of burglary profiles applied in active police investigations. *Criminal Justice and Behavior, 42,* 156–175.

Fox, B., & Farrington, D. P. (2016). Behavioral consistency among serial burglars: Evaluating offense style specialization using three analytical approaches. *Crime & Delinquency, 62,* 1123–1158.

Fox, B., & Farrington, D. P. (2018). What have we learned from offender profiling? A systematic review and meta-analysis of 40 years of research. *Psychological Bulletin, 144*(12), 1247–1274.

Geberth, V. J. (1990). The serial killer and the revelations of Ted Bundy. *Law and Order, 38*(5), 72–77.

Goodwill, A. M., Alison, L. J., & Beech, A. R. (2009). What works in offender profiling? A comparison of typological, thematic, and multivariate models. *Behavioral Sciences & the Law, 27*(4), 507–529.

Goodwin, M., & Canter, D. (1997). Encounters of death: The spatial behavior of U.S. serial killers. *Policing: An International Journal, 20*(1), 24–38.

Guttman, L. (1954). A new approach to factor analysis: The radex. In P. F. Lazarsfeld (Ed.), *Mathematical thinking in the social sciences* (pp. 258–348). Glencoe, IL: Free Press.

Hazelwood, R. R., & Burgess, A. W. (Eds.). (1987). *Practical aspects of rape investigation: A multidisciplinary approach.* New York, NY: Elsevier.

Hazelwood, R. R., & Douglas, J. E. (1980, April). The lust murderer. *FBI Law Enforcement Bulletin*, 1–5.

Hazelwood, R. R., & Michaud, S. (2001). *The evil that men do: FBI profiler Roy Hazelwood's journey into the minds of sexual predators.* New York, NY: Scribner.

Hicks, S. J., & Sales, B. D. (2006). *Criminal profiling: Developing an effective science and practice.* Washington, DC: American Psychological Association.

Holmes, R. M., & Holmes, S. T. (1996). *Profiling violent crimes: An investigative tool.* Thousand Oaks, CA: Sage.

Holmes, R. M., & Holmes, S. T. (2002). *Profiling violent crimes: An investigative tool* (3rd ed.). Thousand Oaks, CA: Sage.

Howitt, D. (2002). *Forensic and criminal psychology.* Harlow: Pearson Education.

Kapardis, A. (1989). One hundred armed robbers in Melbourne: Myths and reality. In D. Challinger (Ed.), *Armed robbery* (pp. 37–47). Canberra, Australia: Australian Institute of Criminology.

Kocsis, R. N. (2003). Criminal psychological profiling: Validities and abilities. *International Journal of Offender Therapy and Comparative Criminology, 47*(2), 126–144.

Kocsis, R. N. (2004). Psychological profiling of serial arson offenses: An assessment of skills and accuracy. *Criminal Justice and Behavior, 31*(3), 341–361.

Kocsis, R. N. (2006). Validities and abilities in criminal profiling: The dilemma for David Canter's investigative psychology. *International Journal of Offender Therapy and Comparative Criminology, 50*(4), 458–477.

Kocsis, R. N. (2013). The criminal profiling reality: What is actually behind the smoke and mirrors? *Journal of Forensic Psychology Practice, 13*(2), 79–91.

Kocsis, R. N. (2015). *The name of the rose* and criminal profiling: The benefits of ViCAP and ViCLAS. *Journal of Forensic Psychology Practice, 15*, 58–79.

Kocsis, R. N., & Cooksey, R. W. (2002). Criminal psychological profiling of serial arson crimes. *International Journal of Offender Therapy and Comparative Criminology, 46*, 631–656.

Kocsis, R. N., Hayes, A. F., & Irwin, H. J. (2002). Investigative experience and accuracy in psychological profiling of a violent crime. *Journal of Interpersonal Violence, 17*(8), 811–823.

Kocsis, R. N., Irwin, H. J., & Hayes, A. F. (1998). Organised and disorganised behaviour syndromes in arsonists: A validation study of a psychological profiling concept. *Psychiatry, Psychology and Law, 5*, 117–130.

Kocsis, R. N., Middledorp, J., & Karpin, A. (2008). Taking stock of accuracy in criminal profiling: The theoretical quandary for investigative psychology. *Journal of Forensic Psychology Practice*, *8*(3), 244–261.

Kocsis, R. N., & Palermo, G. B. (2015). Disentangling criminal profiling: Accuracy, homology, and the myth of trait-based profiling. *International Journal of Offender Therapy and Comparative Criminology*, *59*(3), 1–20.

Pinizzotto, A. J. (1984). Forensic psychology: Criminal personality profiling. *Journal of Police Science & Administration*, *12*, 32–39.

Rainbow, L. (2011a). Professionalising the process. In L. Alison & L. Rainbow (Eds.), *Professionalizing offender profiling: Forensic and investigative psychology in practice* (pp. 1–3). London: Routledge.

Rainbow, L. (2011b). Taming the beast: The UK approach to the management of behavioural investigative advice. In L. Alison & L. Rainbow (Eds.), *Professionalizing offender profiling: Forensic and investigative psychology in practice* (pp. 6–17). London: Routledge.

Rainbow, L., & Gregory, A. (2011). What behavioural investigative advisers actually do. In L. Alison & L. Rainbow (Eds.), *Professionalizing offender profiling: Forensic and investigative psychology in practice* (pp. 18–34). London: Routledge.

Reppetto, T. A. (1974). *Residential crime*. Cambridge, MA: Ballinger.

Ressler, R. K., Burgess, A. W., & Douglas, J. E. (1988). *Sexual homicide: Patterns and motives*. Lexington, MA: Lexington Books.

Ressler, R. K., & Schachtman, T. (1992). *Whoever fights monsters*. New York, NY: St. Martin's Press.

Rossmo, D. K. (1995). *Geographic profiling: Target patterns of serial murderers* (Unpublished Doctoral Dissertation), Simon Fraser University, Burnaby, British Columbia, Canada.

Rossmo, D. K. (1997). Geographic profiling. In J. L. Jackson & D. A. Bekerian (Eds.), *Offender profiling: Theory, research and practice* (pp. 159–176). Chichester: John Wiley & Sons.

Rossmo, D. K. (2000). *Geographic profiling*. Roca Raton, FL: CRC Press.

Salfati, C. G., & Canter, D. V. (1999). Differentiating stranger murders: Profiling offender characteristics from behavioral styles. *Behavioral Sciences and the Law*, *17*(3), 391–406.

Santtila, P., Pakkanen, T., Zappala, A., Bosco, D., Valkama, M., & Mokros, A. (2008). Behavioural crime linking in serial homicide. *Psychology, Crime and Law*, *14*(3), 245–265.

Snook, B., Cullen, R. M., Bennell, C., Taylor, P. J., & Gendreau, P. (2008). The criminal profiling illusion: What's behind the smoke and mirrors? *Criminal Justice & Behavior*, *35*, 1257–1276.

State v. Stevens. (2001). Tennessee 78 S.W. 817.

Steadman, H. J., Silver, E., Monahan, J., Appelbaum, P. S., Robbins, P. C., Mulvey, E. P., . . . Banks, S. (2000). A classification tree approach to the development of actuarial violence risk assessment tools. *Law and Human Behavior*, *24*, 83–100.

Stevens, J. A. (1997). Standard investigatory tools and offender profiling. In J. L. Jackson & D. A. Bekerian (Eds.), *Offender profiling: Theory, research and practice* (pp. 77–106). Chichester: John Wiley & Sons.

Sturidsson, K., Långström, N., Grann, M., Sjöstedt, G., Åsgård, U., & Aghede, E. M. (2006). Using multidimensional scaling for the analysis of sexual offence behaviour: A replication and some cautionary notes. *Psychology, Crime & Law*, *12*(3), 221–230.

Sturidsson, K., Långström, N., Grann, M., Sjöstedt, G., Åsgård, U., & Aghede, E. M. (2009). MDS use with crime scene data replicates poorly: Response to Goodwill, Alison, and Humann (this issue) and Davis (this issue). *Psychology, Crime & Law*, *15*(6), 525–529.

Sugden, P. (1995). *The complete history of Jack the ripper*. London; Carroll & Graf.

Takane, Y., Young, F. W., & De Leeuw, J. (1977). Nonmetric individual differences multidimensional scaling: An alternating least squares method with optimal scaling features. *Psychometrika*, *42*(1), 7–67.

Torres, A. N., Boccanccini, M. T., & Miller, H. (2006). Perceptions of the validity and utility of criminal profiling among forensic psychologists and psychiatrists. *Professional Psychology Research and Practice*, *37*, 51–58.

Trager, J., & Brewster, J. (2001). The effectiveness of psychological profiles. *Journal of Police and Criminal Psychology*, *16*, 20–28.

Turvey, B. E. (Ed.). (2011). *Criminal profiling: An introduction to behavioral evidence analysis*. San Diego, CA: Elsevier, Academic Press.

3 Progress towards evidence-based offender profiling

Introduction

Chapter 2 traced the development of offender profiling and reviewed classic cases such as Jack the Ripper, the Yorkshire Ripper, and the Mad Bomber of New York City. However, none of these cases, or other cases before the 1980s, used evidence-based offender profiling (EBOP). Instead, they were based on intuition or clinical knowledge about the types of people who were likely to commit particular types of crimes.

As an example, offender profiling, as originally developed by the Federal Bureau of Investigation's (FBI) Behavioral Science Unit in the 1970s, was essentially clinical in nature (see Hazelwood & Burgess, 1987; Ressler, Burgess, & Douglas, 1988). Its aim was to analyze the behavior of the offender, understand the motive for the offense, and hence infer what type of person had committed the offense. This inference was based on the experience and expertise of the profiler.

The use of FBI profiles increased greatly over the years. Between 1971 and 1981, the FBI provided profiling assistance on 192 occasions (Pinizzotto, 1984). A few years later, Douglas and Burgess (1986) reported that FBI profiles had been asked to assist with about 600 criminal investigations per year. Later, according to Witkin (1996), profiling assistance was provided by 12 FBI profilers in approximately 1,000 cases per year.

In the United Kingdom, the clinical approach to offender profiling was set out by Copson, Badcock, Boon, and Britton (1997). It aimed to establish what happened, where, when, how, and to whom. It aimed to reconstruct the events and infer the offender's motivation. It searched for underlying psychological influences, including the offender's emotions, moods, desires, and obsessions. Based on their clinical experience and expertise and on their knowledge of relevant literature, profilers provided advice to the police about the likely characteristics (a "psychological signature") of the offender.

Copson (1995) carried out an extensive review of the early use of offender profiling by British police forces. He collected information on 184 cases (predominantly of murder or rape) in which profiling had been used, from 48 different police departments. He reported a considerable increase in the use of profiling, from 25 cases in 1992 to 45 in 1993 and 75 in 1994. However, Copson found that profiling helped to solve the case only 14% of the time and helped identify the offender in only 3% of cases. Nevertheless, respondents said that it helped the police to understand the offender in 61% of cases, reassured officers about their own judgment in 52% of cases, and was considered to be operationally useful in 83% of cases. Similarly, in the United States, Pinizzotto (1984) found that while 77% of surveyed police officers regarded a profile as useful in focusing their investigation, only 17% thought that the profile had actually assisted in the identification of the offender.

In the United Kingdom, a statistical approach to offender profiling was pioneered by David Canter. He used geographic profiling to help the police to catch and convict John Duffy, the "railway murderer," in 1988. Canter examined the details of each crime and built up a picture of the attacker's personality and habits. By noting where the attacks took place, Canter was able to predict where the offender was living (within a circle containing the locations of attacks in London). After the trial, it was stated that 13 of Canter's 17 predictions about the attacker's lifestyle and habits were correct (see Canter, 1994). After this case, it was stated that Canter had been asked to provide profiles for over 150 police investigations (up to 2004).

Canter (2019) then developed offender profiling into the larger field of investigative psychology (IP). This was based on his work on geographic profiling, which identified that offenders tended to commit crimes close to their homes, and that the offenders' homes tended to lie within the area that was circumscribed by the crimes. Canter also argued that criminal actions were based on four types of narratives: professional, adventure, victim, and tragedy. For example, many burglaries by young offenders involved adventure, while many homicides were described as tragedies by their perpetrators. In addition to profiling, Canter argued that IP included methods of linking crimes to one offender, detecting deception, investigative interviewing, eyewitness identification, and police decision making.

Richard Kocsis has also been an influential pioneer of offender profiling, and he recently reviewed this topic in the *Sage Encyclopedia of Criminal Psychology* (Kocsis, 2019). He pointed out that, in profiling, features of the crime are assessed in order to develop a template of descriptive features of the likely perpetrator. However, he considered that the validity and utility of profiling had not been convincingly demonstrated. There were anecdotal accounts and case examples, demonstrations that profilers could predict the characteristics of unknown offenders in exercises based on previously solved cases, and surveys of police personnel about the utility of profiling. But what is needed is a randomized trial in which real-life, unsolved cases are randomly assigned to receive profiling or not in order to investigate whether cases involving profiling are more likely to be solved than other cases. This was proposed by Homant and Kennedy (1998), but such a trial has never yet been conducted.

The Nottinghamshire statistical profiling research

In an effort to advance the statistical basis of offender profiling, Farrington and Lambert (1997, 2000, 2007) carried out research in the 1990s based on police records of 655 different (burglary and violent) offenders who had been convicted during a nine-month period but in which the identity of the offender at the time of the offense was not known by victims, witnesses, or the police. Obviously, problems of detecting offenders do not arise when someone knows the offender (as is true in the majority of cases of violence, which involve acquaintances, relatives, friends, or intimate cohabitees). In the Nottinghamshire police records, a victim or witness knew the identity of the offender in 74.1% of violence cases but in only 6.6% of burglary cases.

All the offenses included in this project involved offenders who were strangers to the victim. The main aim of the research was to investigate statistical regularities between types of offenders and types of offenses, types of victims, and reports by victims and witnesses.

The most common ways in which burglars were arrested were that they were caught in the act (14.5%); through an informant (12.5%); they were caught near to or leaving the scene of the crime (12.0%); they were traced through property left at the scene of the crime or through the disposal of stolen goods (10.5%); they were seen acting suspiciously in the area, for example, carrying stolen goods (7.7%); they were caught for another crime and admitted the burglary (7.0%); or through an accurate description by a witness (6.7%). The most common ways in which violent offenders were arrested were that they were detained at the scene of the crime (16.0%), through an accurate description by a victim (14.7%) or witness (13.3%), through a description of a vehicle or a number plate (10.6%), they were caught in the act (10.6%), or as a result of enquiries in the local area (6.6%). Victim and witness descriptions were much more important in apprehending violent offenders than burglars, no doubt because violent offenders were more often seen by victims and witnesses.

Interestingly, 89.2% of burglars and 79.1% of violent offenders had a previous criminal record (before their current arrest). This suggests that the vast majority of persons who commit unsolved crimes can be found in police records. Just over half of the burglars (51.1%) had one or more previous burglaries, in comparison with about a quarter (25.1%) of the violent offenders. Similarly, nearly half of the violent offenders (46.8%) had at least one previous violent offense, in comparison with about one-third (32.4%) of the burglars. As many as 36.2% of burglars and 23.6% of violent offenders had 10 or more previous convictions.

Characteristics of the offenders were recorded on the police description and antecedent history forms that were completed at the time of the arrest. In the 1990s, these forms were not routinely computerized, but they were computerized by the researchers (i.e. Farrington and Lambert). Not surprisingly, most offenders were male (95.4% of burglars, 90.6% of violent). Most offenders were white (88.9%), with 5.6% described as African Caribbean, 4.2% of mixed race, and 1.3% Asian. Most offenders were aged 17 to 24 (56.5% of burglars, 51.9% of violent) and had a height between 5 feet, 6 inches and 5 feet, 11 inches (62.7% of burglars, 64.4% of violent). Most offenders lived in the city of Nottingham (56.4% of burglars, 53.0% of violent) rather than in the rest of the county. Many other features were recorded on the forms, including weight, build, hair color, hair length, hair style, facial hair, eye color, voice, accent, and tattoos; 36.5% of burglars and 39.6% of violent offenders were tattooed.

Unfortunately, some of these features were not reliably coded, although, of course, some could change over time. It was possible to compare 177 cases where two forms were completed for the same offender, because of two separate arrests. Among the most reliably recorded features were sex (100% agreement), accent (97.0%), ethnicity (96.4%), facial hair (92.5%), age (86.7%), hair length (86.5%), tattoos (84.8%), and eye color (82.6%). Among the least reliably recorded (or more changeable) features were voice (46.4%), hair color (54.7%), height (69.5%), weight (73.1%), build (77.3%), and address (77.6%). Ideally, for an offender profile to be useful, it is desirable that features should stay constant over time.

Many offense features were related to offender features, in the 1,017 offense–offender pairs. For example, most burglary (69.2%) and violent (55.3%) offenders lived within one mile of the scene of the crime. Only 8.1% of burglars and 14.8% of violent offenders lived more than five miles from the scene of the crime. Therefore, the location of the offense was an important clue to the address of the offender.

Location (city versus county), site (street versus other), time (night versus day), and day (weekday versus weekend) were used to create offense profiles. Address (city versus county), age (21 or over versus 20 or less), sex (male versus female), and ethnicity (white versus non-white) were used to create offender profiles. Some offense profiles were clearly related to some offender profiles. For example, for violence when the offense occurred in the street in the city at night-time (6pm–6am) on a weekday

(Monday–Thursday), the offenders tended to be older white males living in the city. For city offenses in other places in daytime on a weekday, the offenders tended to be older white or non-white city males. For city offenses in other places in daytime on a weekend (Friday–Sunday), the offenders tended to be younger non-white city females or older white city males. Overall, 41.1% of predictions of offender profiles based on offense profiles were correct in a validation sample.

Farrington and Lambert (2007) also investigated the prediction of offender profiles from victim profiles. This analysis was based on 1,084 offender–victim pairs. For violence, the address–age–sex profile of the victim was compared with the address-age-sex-ethnicity profile of the offender. (The victim's ethnicity was rarely recorded explicitly – in only 14.8% of cases.) Overall, 51.1% of offender profiles based on victim profiles were correct in a validation sample. Farrington and Lambert (1997) also studied the prediction of age–sex–ethnicity profiles of violent offenders according to victim and witness descriptions. These analyses were based on 417 victim–offender pairs and 315 witness–offender pairs. On average, 45.9% of age–sex–ethnicity profiles reported by victims were correct, as were 53.7% of these profiles reported by witnesses.

This analysis of statistical regularities between offenses, offenders, victims, and victim and witness reports was an important development towards EBOP. The researchers wanted to follow up these analyses by using the offender profiles operationally with Nottinghamshire police; however, the Home Office declined to fund any further research based on "volume" offenses because it had taken a policy decision to only fund offender profiling research on serious offenses such as homicide and rape. Happily, Fox and Farrington (2012, 2015) then carried out the next level of EBOP research in Florida, and this is described in Chapter 4.

Knowledge gained from offender profiling

Research on offender profiling was first reviewed by Dowden, Bennell, and Bloomfield (2007) and Snook, Eastwood, Gendreau, Goggin, and Cullen (2007). However, the most recent and extensive review was conducted by Fox and Farrington (2018). They aimed to review all publications on offender profiling from 1976 to 2016. They found 513 publications but excluded 87 that were on the very specialized topic of geographic profiling, so their main analyses were based on the remaining 426 publications.

The most common types of publications were on profile development (31.7%) and a general discussion of profiling (31.4%). Only 5.2% compared different methods, and only 9.4% tried to evaluate profiles empirically. The most common types of authors were psychologists (42.7%), criminologists (17.0%), and law enforcement or government (9.8%). The most prolific authors were Richard Kocsis (30 publications), David Canter (n = 24), and Laurence Alison (n = 24). The most popular journal outlets were the *Journal of Investigative Psychology and Offender Profiling* (33 publications), the *International Journal of Offender Therapy and Comparative Criminology* (n = 25), and the *FBI Law Enforcement Bulletin* (n = 20). Then number of publications increased dramatically over time, from 19 in 1976–1985 to 59 in 1986–1995, 150 in 1996–2005, and 198 in 2006–2016. The use of advanced statistics also increased over time. In 1976–1985, 68% of publications (n = 13) used no statistical analysis, 32% of publications (n = 6) used basic descriptive statistics, and no publications used advanced statistics. In contrast, in 2006–2016, only 40% of publications (n = 80) used no statistical analysis, 26% (n = 52) used basic descriptive statistics, and 33% (n = 66) used advanced statistics. Over time, the proportion of authors from the FBI decreased from 45% in 1976–1985 (n = 13) to zero in 2006–2016. Similarly, the proportion of authors from other law enforcement agencies decreased from 24% in 1976–1985 (n = 7) to 9% in 2006–2016 (n = 40). The largest increase in publications occurred among psychologists, who authored only 5 articles in 1976–1985 but nearly 200 articles (counting author–article combinations) in 2006–2016.

The most common specific crime types that were studied in offender profiling publications were homicide (26.5%), sexual assault (13.4%), and burglary (5.2%). Nearly half of all publications (41.5%) were more general and did not focus on a specific type of crime. In total, 62 publications reported specific profiles, including 14 on homicide, 14 on sexual assault, 11 on sexual homicide, 8 on arson, and 4 on burglary. Burglary profiles were published by Farrington and Lambert (1997); Merry and Harsent (2000); Santtila, Ritvanen, and Mokros (2004); and Fox and Farrington (2012).

For homicide, the recurring profiles were expressive or emotional, instrumental (for financial gain or revenge), and visionary (in response to visions). For sexual assault, the recurring profiles were hostility, opportunistic, disorganized, and power-control. For sexual homicide, the recurring profiles were sadistic, sexual, organized, disorganized, anger-fury, and power-control. For arson, the recurring profiles were expressive, instrumental, revenge, and crime concealment. For burglary, the recurring profiles were organized versus disorganized. Chapter 4 discusses burglary profiles in detail.

While there has been a great increase in publications on offender profiling in the past 40 years and a great increase in statistical rigor, what is largely missing is the implementation of profiles in police investigations and the evaluation of their effects on arrest rates in unsolved cases using an experimental design. Chapter 4 describes the most important example so far of this kind of implementation and evaluation. In the future, cost–benefit analyses of the implementation of offender profiles should be carried out, based on previous cost–benefit analyses in criminology (see, e.g., Welsh, Farrington, & Sherman, 2001; Welsh, Farrington, & Gowar, 2015).

References

Canter, D. (1994). *Criminal shadows: Inside the mind of the serial killer*. London: Harper Collins.

Canter, D. (2019). Investigative psychology. In R. D. Morgan (Ed.), *The Sage encyclopedia of criminal psychology* (pp. 706–708). Thousand Oaks, CA: Sage.

Copson, G. (1995). *Coals to Newcastle? Police use of offender profiling*. London: Home Office Police Department.

Copson, G., Badcock, R., Boon, J., & Britton, P. (1997). Articulating a systematic approach to clinical crime profiling. *Criminal Behaviour and Mental Health, 7*, 13–17.

Douglas, J. E., & Burgess, A. W. (1986, December). Criminal profiling: A viable investigative tool against violent crime. *FBI Law Enforcement Bulletin, 55*, 9–13.

Dowden, C., Bennell, C., & Bloomfield, S. (2007). Advances in offender profiling: A systematic review of the profiling literature published over the past three decades. *Journal of Police and Criminal Psychology, 22*, 44–56.

Farrington, D. P., & Lambert, S. (1997). Predicting offender profiles from victim and witness descriptions. In J. L. Jackson & D. A. Bekerian (Eds.), *Offender profiling: Theory, research and practice* (pp. 133–158). Chichester: John Wiley & Sons.

Farrington, D. P., & Lambert, S. (2000). Statistical approaches to offender profiling. In D. V. Canter & L. J. Alison (Eds.), *Profiling property crimes* (pp. 235–273). Abingdon: Ashgate Publishing.

Farrington, D. P., & Lambert, S. (2007). Predicting offender profiles from offense and victim characteristics. In R. N. Kocsis (Ed.), *Criminal profiling: International theory, research and practice* (pp. 135–167). Totowa, NJ: Humana Press.

Fox, B., & Farrington, D. P. (2012). Creating burglary profiles using latent class analysis: A new approach to offender profiling. *Criminal Justice and Behavior, 39*, 1582–1611.

Fox, B., & Farrington, D. P. (2015). An experimental evaluation on the utility of burglary profiles applied in active police investigations. *Criminal Justice and Behavior, 42*, 156–175.

Fox, B., & Farrington, D. P. (2018). What have we learned from offender profiling? A systematic review and meta-analysis of 40 years of research. *Psychological Bulletin, 144*, 1247–1274.

Hazelwood, R. R., & Burgess, A. W. (Eds.). (1987). *Practical aspects of rape investigation*. Amsterdam, Netherlands: Elsevier.

Homant, R. J., & Kennedy, D. B. (1998). Psychological aspects of crime scene profiling: Validity research. *Criminal Justice and Behavior, 25*, 319–343.

Kocsis, R. N. (2019). Criminal profiling. In R. D. Morgan (Ed.), *The Sage encyclopedia of criminal psychology* (pp. 267–269). Thousand Oaks, CA: Sage.

Merry, S., & Harsent, L. (2000). Intruders, pilferers, raiders and invaders: The interpersonal dimension of burglary. In D. V. Canter & L. J. Alison (Eds.), *Profiling property crimes* (pp. 31–57). Aldershot: Ashgate Publishing.

Pinizzotto, A. J. (1984). Forensic psychology: Criminal personality profiling. *Journal of Police Science and Administration, 12*, 32–40.

Ressler, R. K., Burgess, A. W., & Douglas, J. E. (1988). *Sexual homicide: Patterns and motives*. Lexington, MA: Lexington Books.

Santtila, P., Ritvanen, A., & Mokros, A. (2004). Predicting burglar characteristics from crime scene behavior. *International Journal of Police Science and Management, 6*, 136–154.

Snook, B., Eastwood, J., Gendreau, P., Goggin, C., & Cullen, R. M. (2007). Taking stock of criminal profiling: A narrative review and meta-analysis. *Criminal Justice and Behavior, 34*, 437–453.

Welsh, B. C., Farrington, D. P., & Gowar, B. R. (2015). Benefit-cost analysis of crime prevention programs. In M. Tonry (Ed.), *Crime and justice* (Vol. 44, pp. 447–516). Chicago: University of Chicago Press.

Welsh, B. C., Farrington, D. P., & Sherman, L. W. (Eds.). (2001). *Costs and benefits of preventing crime*. Boulder, CO: Westview Press.

Witkin, G. (1996, April 22). How the FBI paints portraits of the nation's most wanted. *US News and World Report, 120*, 32.

4 Evidence-based offender profiles and evaluations in the United States

Introduction

As noted throughout this book, offender profiling has achieved unprecedented fame and credibility as a policing practice across the globe (with hundreds of movies, TV shows, books, magazine articles, and elevated status in pop culture), despite very little science and evaluation unpinning the practice (Dowden, Bennell, & Bloomfield, 2007; Fox & Farrington, 2018; Jackson, van Koppen, & Herbrink, 1993; Kocsis, 2007). In fact, one of the first published articles on offender profiling, written in 1976 by the editor of *Psychology Today*, questioned whether profilers are any "better than bartenders" in predicting the personality traits and features of an unidentified person based upon limited crime scene information (Campbell, 1976).

Luckily, in the four decades since that article was published, there has been considerable advancement in the field of offender profiling, with new cutting-edge research informed by statistical and scientific approaches to offender profiling (Dowden et al., 2007; Fox & Farrington, 2018). The goal of this chapter is to provide a detailed definition and explanation of one such method, called evidence-based offender profiling (EBOP) (Fox & Farrington, 2012, 2015), and overview the profiles that have been developed thus far using this new scientific method. Specifically, the chapter discusses how EBOP overcomes many issues faced by the more subjective clinical profiling methods, such as low accuracy and effectiveness, when used in police investigations. This chapter also provides a "step-by-step" guide to conducting EBOP, so that replication and proliferation of the method may occur, and so that the field of offender profiling and those that it impacts may benefit from this more scientific methodological approach.

The need for evidence-based offender profiling

Offender profiling has historically been difficult to evaluate, given the multiple definitions, approaches, and even measures of success that have been proposed in the field (Dowden et al., 2007; Fox & Farrington, 2018). For instance, some practitioners and academics adhere to a more traditional definition of offender profiling, and consider it to be a technique used to identify the major personality, behavioral, and demographic characteristics of an offender based on an analysis of the crimes that he or she has committed (Douglas, Ressler, Burgess, & Hartman, 1986). Additional definitions and subsequent approaches to offender profiling include criminal investigative analysis (CIA), developed by the FBI's Behavioral Science Unit (BSU) (Douglas et al., 1986), investigative psychology developed by David Canter (Canter, 1995), geographic profiling developed by Kim Rossmo (Rossmo, 1999), and many more. Some of these approaches develop profiles through the use of rigorous statistical methods and quantitative data, while others are subjectively created by profilers based upon their "experience, intuition, and educated guesswork" (Geberth, 1990, p. 492; Pinizzotto, 1984, p. 33).

Until recently, Campbell's (1976) notable question on the accuracy of offender profiling largely went unanswered, with few tests being conducted to measure how accurate various profiling methods were in predicting traits of unknown offenders, and how much impact offender profiling had when applied in the field. As accurately summarized by Snook and colleagues (2009), "we need evidence that [offender profiling] works" (p. 1092). Extant research on the accuracy and utility of offender profiling, while limited, does indicate some clear trends worth noting. These findings are described in the sections to follow.

Evaluations of clinical profiling methods

As noted and described in Chapter 2 of this book, clinical profiling is an approach to offender profiling whereby profiles are developed on a case-by-case basis by a profiler who has considerable training, experience, and practice in the field, but with no clear and replicable process, methodology, data, or statistical analysis outlined or utilized in the development of the profiles (see, e.g., Douglas et al., 1986; Holmes & Holmes, 1996). The most famous example of clinical profiling is from the FBI's BSU, which is best known for developing the field of offender profiling in the 1970s and 1980s after conducting interviews with 36 of the most infamous serial killers, murderers, and rapists in the nation (Ted Bundy, John Wayne Gacy, Charles Manson, Sirhan Sirhan, and more). Based upon these interviews and the experience of the FBI Special Agents in the BSU, profiles were developed of the demographic, personality, and behavioral characteristics of offenders who were responsible for committing serial murder, rape, and arson (Douglas, Burgess, Burgess, & Ressler, 1992; Hazelwood & Burgess, 1987; Ressler, Burgess, & Douglas, 1988).

While the FBI's approach has become wildly popular in the media and mainstream society, these profiles have come under scrutiny in recent years as they were created using anecdotal evidence, not quantitative data and statistical methods (see, e.g., Kocsis & Cooksey, 2002; Snook et al., 2009). Additionally, evaluations of these (and other) clinical approaches to offender profiling have yielded less than stellar results.

For instance, Pinizzotto (1984) used a "consumer satisfaction survey" methodology to evaluate the 192 profiles created by the FBI between 1971 and 1981. He asked the police who used these profiles to rate how useful they were in their investigations and whether they helped or harmed the investigation. Results indicated that fewer than half of all the cases profiled by the FBI were solved (n = 88), and just 17% of the police stated that the profiles directly aided in the identification of a suspect (Pinizzotto, 1984). Moreover, another 17% responded that that FBI's profiles "were not useful at all" (Pinizzotto, 1984). In a follow-up study, Jackson et al. (1993) asked police officers in The Netherlands about the utility of profiles provided to them by an FBI-trained profiler. While the sample size was low (n = 6), two officers (33%) thought that the profiles were very useful, three thought they were reasonably useful, and one (17%) thought that they were not useful. However, not a single officer stated that the profiles that they received from FBI trained profilers helped them identify the offender or solve the case.

Similar results were found when evaluating other clinically derived profiles across the globe. In the United Kingdom, Copson (1995) found that 3% of the evaluated profiles helped identify the offender, 14% said that the profiles helped the case ultimately to get solved, and 16% said that they helped to open new lines of inquiry. Trager and Brewster (2001) found that among 48 surveyed police officers in the United States, 38% believed that the clinical profiles they used directly assisted in the identification of a suspect, though 25% said that the profiles had actually hindered their investigation in some way. In Canada, Snook, Taylor and Bennell (2007) found that of the 29 police officers who used a clinically derived profile, 14% thought that the profile helped focus the investigation, 10% said that it led to a better understanding of the suspect, and 3% said that they thought that the profiles provided accurate predictions about the responsible offender.

While these studies have generally not corresponded to the perceived accuracy and utility of offender profiling (which is stereotypically clinical in nature), there are limitations to the consumer satisfaction evaluation model, as police satisfaction with profiles is not necessarily proof of the true accuracy of offender profiling (Jeffers, 1991; Kocsis & Palermo, 2007; *State v. Stevens*, 2001; US House of Representatives, 1990). A study by Alison, Smith, and Morgan (2003) helped demonstrate this, as the researchers asked police to rate the accuracy of two profiles, though one was "real" and one was "fake" (i.e., developed by the lead author of the study). However, results showed that police rated both profiles as equally accurate (Alison et al., 2003). Studies have also found a positive relationship between a person's initial belief in the accuracy of offender profiling and her or his future perceived accuracy of a profile (Kocsis & Hayes, 2004; Kocsis & Heller, 2004; Kocsis & Middledorp, 2004). In other words, the more someone initially believes in the accuracy of profiling, the more likely that she or he will perceive profiles to be correct and useful in the future (Kocsis & Middledorp, 2004). Therefore, these evaluations may actually over-inflate the accuracy of clinical derived profiles, such as those developed by the FBI.

In the only evaluation of the effects of clinically derived profiles on case clearance (i.e., not perceptually based), carried out by the British Home Office in the 1990s (Gudjonsson & Copson, 1997), the researchers found that, of the 184 profiled cases, the profiles directly led to an arrest in five cases, and hence that there was only a 2.7% success rate when the profiles were actually applied in the field.

Evaluations of statistical profiling methods

In contrast to the clinical profiling approach, statistical offender profiling is based upon statistical regularities found between the way that certain offenses are committed and the features of responsible offenders based upon objective analysis of large datasets of crimes (Fox & Farrington, 2018). This scientific approach has been growing in popularity in the offender profiling field (see, e.g., Bennell & Canter, 2002; Canter, 1995; Farrington & Lambert, 2000; Fox & Farrington, 2012), and it has many advantages in terms of replicability, data-driven findings, and increased accuracy and utility when applied in the field.

The first to propose a more statistical approach to offender profiling was David Canter, who in 1995 suggested that offender profiling is founded on the "A to C equation", in which A represents the actions involved in a crime known to the police (e.g., crime location, method of entry, state of scene) and C refers to the characteristics of the responsible offender (e.g., criminal history, identifying traits). Specifically, Canter believed that profiles of offender characteristics could be developed and linked statistically to actions involved in a crime using a database of known offenses and offenders. When features of crimes committed by different individuals are similar, he thought that the offenders who committed those crimes must also share some common underlying traits, which can also be generalized to other unknown perpetrators of similar crime styles to aid in their identification (Canter, 1995; Holmes & Holmes, 1996). Through the use of statistical analysis of crime and offender data, unique sub-types of offenses and offenders can be developed and statistically linked together to develop more scientifically informed offender profiles.

Another example of a statistically based approach to offender profiling is crime linkage analysis (CLA). CLA, which was first conducted by Bennell and Canter (2002), aims to statistically link crimes to a single offender on the basis of various crime scene behaviors and evaluates the accuracy of the linking decisions made. CLA is typically based upon receiver operating characteristic (ROC) analysis to evaluate behavioral similarity across offenses and determine the likelihood of case linkage (Bennell, Mugford, Ellingwood, & Woodhams, 2014). Next, an area under the ROC curve (AUC) analysis is used to determine the accuracy of the decision to link crimes to a serial offender (Bennell et al., 2014; Steadman et al., 2000). Given the statistical sophistication of CLA, this approach has been a rapidly growing area in the offender profiling field.

A recent meta-analysis of the accuracy of CLA was conducted by Fox and Farrington (2018), based upon 34 effect sizes derived from 18 studies identified using a thorough search of electronic databases and references for published literature on CLA from 2002 through 2016. Results of the meta-analysis indicated that CLA has been performed on five crime types (homicide, sex offenses, burglary, robbery, and car theft) using data from six different countries (United Kingdom, Canada, United States, Finland, South Africa, and Japan) and samples ranging in size from 49 to 720 offenses (Fox & Farrington, 2018). Most important, this meta-analysis indicated that the weighted mean effect size for all CLA studies was AUC = 0.83, suggesting that, overall, CLA models are highly accurate in linking crimes in a series to a single offender. Indeed, 18% of the examined effect sizes indicated near perfect accuracy when linking crimes together (AUC = 0.90 to 1.00), and 62% were highly accurate (AUC = 0.70 to 0.89) (Swets, 1988).

While this finding is very positive for the accuracy of statistical profiling methods, it applies only to CLA and not to more typical forms of offender profiling. In that realm, few evaluations have been conducted, and while more methodologically advanced, few statistical approaches to offender profiling advocate for the use of a scientific evaluation component to be integrated into the methodology.

Evidence-based offender profiling

Given the methodological and philosophical superiority of statistical profiling methods, as well as the lack of empirical evaluation and replication of existing statistically derived profiles, Fox and Farrington (2012, 2015) established the evidenced-based offender profiling (EBOP) approach.

EBOP advocates for the use of objective statistical classification techniques, such as latent class analysis (LCA) and related "person-focused" analytical methods with objective goodness-of-fit criteria and conditional item probabilities, which provide quantitative information on the number and composition of resulting sub-types, and allows cases with a specific pattern to be assigned to a resulting sub-type (Fox & Farrington, 2012). Specifically, LCA aims to identify the fewest number of sub-types when those in each group are highly similar to each other, but qualitatively different from those in other sub-types, based upon two or more indicator measures (Francis, Bowater, & Soothill, 2004; Muthen & Muthen, 2000).

This analysis eliminates a great deal of subjectivity in offender profiling, specifically because the goodness-of-fit measures objectively indicate the number of sub-types in the data, the quantitative output indicates the precise composition of the resulting sub-types, and the classification probabilities allow researchers to determine sub-type membership for each case in the dataset. LCA is the ideal analytical technique for use in EBOP, as it is fulfills the goals of an objective statistical classification technique, and it has many benefits over related classification methods used in the offender profiling literature.

To conduct an LCA, indicator measures (similar to independent variables) are identified and used to inform the development of the latent classes (i.e., resulting sub-types). Nominal, ordinal, and continuous variables can be used in LCA, though the underlying math informing the LCA and the resulting outcomes will differ depending upon the type of variables that are used. For instance, nominal and ordinal variables produce conditional item probabilities indicating the proportional distribution of each level of the variable across each sub-type, while continuous variables produce mean values for the variable for each resultant sub-type. Finally, numerous class solutions must be evaluated to determine which provides the best fit for the data. Typically, up to nine potential classes are evaluated, though more can be tested if a large dataset or a large number (i.e., more than 10) of indicator measures are used in the LCA.

To determine the ideal number of classes (i.e., resulting sub-types), multiple objective goodness-of-fit criteria are typically evaluated. These criteria include the Akaike information criterion (AIC), the Bayesian information criterion (BIC), and the consistent Akaike information criterion (CAIC) (Uebersax, 2009). Similar to chi-square tests, these criteria indicate the difference between an estimated model and the actual data observations; however, in this analysis, lower values indicate a better fit, as these criteria reward model parsimony. As one class solution will often not produce the lowest values across all three criteria measures, the model with most measures in its favor is selected. An example of LCA goodness-of-fit criteria is shown in Table 4.1.

Table 4.1 Example goodness-of-fit indices for five potential class solutions in LCA

No. of classes	AIC(LL)	BIC(LL)	CAIC(LL)	LL	npar	df	Class error
1	2250.3	2303.5	2314.5	−1612.32	13	362	.0000
2	2195.9	2201.2	2228.2	−2020.57	27	348	.0000
3	2091.9	2062.9	2123.9	−1904.68	41	334	.0283
4	2086.7	**2002.7**	**2057.7**	−1838.34	55	320	.0337
5	**2056.4**	2027.4	2096.4	−1809.20	69	306	.0409

Note: Bold represents the best class solution for the data. LL= log likelihood, npar = number of parameters, df = degrees of freedom.

Once the optimal number of classes is identified, the conditional item probabilities (and mean values, if continuous indicator measures are used) are inspected to evaluate the composition of resulting classes. This helps to understand (and name) each of the latent classes that were identified in the LCA. For instance, in the example of LCA conditional item probabilities shown in Table 4.2, the first resulting class is characterized by a high proportion of the group (99.9%) having no prior criminal record before the current offense, and most offenders did not know the victim. These features are distinct from the remaining latent classes, indicating that individuals with those features are highly similar to each other but also very different from the other sub-types. For more details on how to conduct LCA or interpret goodness-of-fit criteria or conditional item probabilities, see Muthen and Muthen (2000), Fox and Farrington (2012), Uebersax (2009), and Vermunt and Magidson (2005).

After sub-types of offenses and offenders are identified, the next step in the EBOP process is to assign all cases in the dataset to the resulting sub-types of offenses and offenders (if the data are available) and conduct tests of association to determine the extent to which certain types of offenses are committed by certain types of offenders. This step develops the offense-offender profiles. Chi-square tests of association are an ideal method of analysis, as they indicate whether the offense and offender sub-types are statistically associated to a degree more than chance expectation. Column and/or row percentages may also be inspected to determine whether one sub-type of offenders commit an unusually high proportion of one sub-type of offenses (further establishing information for the resulting crime profile).

However, to truly measure the extent to which a specific offense–offender relationship (i.e., one sub-type of offense and one sub-type of offender) is associated more than chance expectation, adjusted standardized residual (ASR) tests should be conducted. ASR values indicate how many standard deviations above or below the expected count an observed count in a cell is. This differs from similar tests in that it takes into account the overall size

Table 4.2 Example conditional item probabilities for a four-class solution in LCA

		Class 1 %	Class 2 %	Class 3 %	Class 4 %
Criminal history	No criminal record	99.9	9.4	3.7	0.9
	Criminal record	0.1	90.6	96.3	99.1
Past total offenses	No prior offenses	99.9	2.1	5.8	0.2
	1–2 prior offenses	0.1	76.7	10.2	8.2
	3+ prior offenses	0.0	21.2	83.9	91.6
Past violent crimes	No prior violence	100	90.9	99.9	68.3
	Prior violent crimes	0.0	9.1	0.1	31.7
Past drug offenses	No prior drug offenses	100	86.0	85.1	60.9
	Prior drug offenses	0.0	13.9	14.9	39.1
Past sex offenses	No prior sex offenses	99.9	92.2	4.8	60.3
	Prior sex offenses	0.1	7.8	95.2	39.7
Age of onset	Age 9–12	5.3	0.1	22.4	64.5
	Age 13–16	56.6	53.8	74.4	27.7
	Age 16+	37.9	46.1	3.2	7.8
Co-offending	Solo offender	43.3	43.5	27.3	77.7
	Co-offenders	56.6	56.5	72.7	22.3
Know victim	Don't know	60.7	58.3	82.3	47.6
	Know victim	39.3	41.7	17.7	52.4
% of sample		40.9	26.0	12.9	20.1

of the sample and gives a better indication of how much the observed count differs from the expected count (Farrington, Snyder, & Finnegan, 1988). ASR values are calculated using the formula:

$$ASR = O - E/\{\sqrt{E} \times \sqrt{[1 - (R/T)][1 - (C/T)]\}},$$

where O = observed number in cell, E = expected number by chance (i.e. $R \times C/T$), R = row total, C = column total, and T = grand total. ASR values that are greater than 1.96 or less than −1.96 are significant at the $p<.05$ level (two-tailed). Whether the ASR value is positive or negative indicates whether the observed cell value is above or below what is expected by chance. From this information, the offense-offender profiles are established, and they can be used in academia and/or police investigations. An example of chi-square tests of association and ASR values calculated for the relationship between sub-types of offenses and offenders identified in LCAs is shown in Table 4.3.

After developing the statistical profile, the next critical steps in the EBOP model are to replicate profiles developed for various crimes using new samples (and even analytical methods), and to measure the effectiveness of the resulting profiles in increasing clearance rates when used in active police investigations using experimental evaluations. Replication of the statistical profiles will help to determine if the profiles developed in one area differ from those in another area and will increase the reliability and confidence in the profiles if consistency across samples and locations can be established. This would also provide insight into the latent classes that exist within different offenses and examine the similarities and differences in behavior exhibited by offenders in otherwise dissimilar crimes.

Finally, applying and evaluating the impact of statistical profiles used in field investigations is advised in the EBOP model, as this will shed light on

Table 4.3 Example chi-square tests of association and adjusted standardized residuals calculated for the relationship between offender and offense sub-types identified using LCAs

Offender sub-type	Offense style				
	1 *Opportunistic*	*2* *Organized*	*3* *Disorganized*	*4* *Interpersonal*	*Total*
1 Impulsive	33 23.7%	38 28.7%	23 24.8%	55* 63.9%	149 33.1%
2 Peer influenced	57* 41.0%	19 14.4%	15 16.1%	9 10.5%	100 22.2%
3 Substance abusers	26 18.8%	12 – 9.1%	53* 57.0%	18 20.9%	106 23.6%
4 Career criminals	23 – 16.5%	63* 47.8%	2 – 2.1%	4 – 4.7%	95 21.1%
Total	139 100%	132 100%	93 100%	86 100%	450 100%

Source: $\chi^2 = 12.11$, p<.05, n = 450.

Note: Column percentages are shown below observed cell counts. *Indicates a positive significant ASR value at the p<.05 level. – Indicates a negative significant ASR value at the p<.05 level.

the utility of the profiles in a law enforcement rather than an academic setting when measured using a high-quality experimental evaluation. While there are several methods of evaluating the effect of new treatments or programs on an outcome, the most reliable and valid method of doing so is through the use of an experimental design (Farrington & Welsh, 2006). Randomized controlled trials (RCTs) are the gold standard in experimental research and the preferred method of evaluating effects, as randomization allows true causality (i.e., knowing that the treatment caused the change in outcome) to be established. Unfortunately, RCTs are typically very difficult to conduct in criminal justice settings, in large part because of the time, resources, and cooperation needed to implement such a design (Farrington & Welsh, 2006; Lösel, 2008). Therefore, a non-randomized experiment commonly used in social science research is the nonequivalent control group design. This high-quality experimental design involves collection of pre- and post-test measures for an outcome (e.g., crime arrest rates) for both the treatment (e.g., using the statistical profiles) and control (e.g., not using the statistical profiles) groups. This design should also include (1) additional covariates to improve matching between the conditions, (2) multiple pre- and post-treatment measures to get more accurate effect size measures, and (3) multiple treatment or control groups for better comparisons. While the lack of randomization prevents causality from being conclusively established using a nonequivalent group design, these three elements address many of the major threats to internal validity. Therefore, an experimental evaluation of the EBOP statistical profiles, implemented in a police department to help increase arrest rates, should be conducted using an RCT or nonequivalent control group experimental design.

Evidence-based offender profiles

This section provides an overview of two studies which developed evidence-based offender profiles, although broader literature includes development of EBOP profiles for burglars, juvenile homicide and sex offenders, cyber offenders, and more. The limitations of the EBOP method, the need for direct replication of EBOP profiles, and related opportunities for future research are discussed.

EBOP burglary profile

In the first study to develop EBOP profiles, Fox and Farrington (2012) used LCA to identify statistical sub-types within offending behaviors and offender traits among solved burglaries that took place in Florida between 2008 and 2009 (n = 405). To do this, offense reports and arrest records of each burglary and responsible offender were collected from the police department, with critical crime scene behaviors and features of the type of person who committed each crime coded for analysis. Importantly, all information used to develop the profiles is available to law enforcement, so police can apply the profiles using information in their databases.

After all data coding took place, LCA was used to statistically identify sub-types of burglaries and classify them into different styles of offenses. LCA was also run on the criminal history and demographic features for each burglar to classify the responsible offenders into distinct sub-types. The results of Fox and Farrington's (2012) study found that four behavioral offending patterns were identified using the LCA, labeled as follows: (1) organized, (2) disorganized, (3) opportunistic, and (4) interpersonal style offenses.

Similar to the FBI's profile for organized homicides, results of the LCA showed that the organized style burglaries are premeditated offenses where foresight and care were taken to reduce risks and increase gains (Fox & Farrington, 2012). The organized burglar typically brings tools to the crime scene (indicating the premeditation and preparation) and is willing to use forced entry to enter a burglary target. This style of burglary is professional, with little or no evidence left behind, little indication of a burglary taking place, and high-value items stolen that often require fencing or a stolen goods network. In contrast, disorganized style burglaries were found to be highly spontaneous and haphazard, with little concern or effort taken to avoid apprehension or prevent evidence from being left behind. These burglars rarely brought a tool to the crime scene, and if a tool was needed, they typically found something (e.g., a large rock, brick) or used their bodies (arms, hands, feet) to force entry. Once inside, the target was usually ransacked, leaving the scene in disarray and providing a clear indication that a burglary took place. Evidence was commonly left behind, and low-value items were often stolen. Residential and commercial locations were commonly targeted by disorganized burglars. The disorganized burglaries were also similar to the FBI's profile for disorganized homicides (Fox & Farrington, 2012).

Two additional profiles for burglary were identified using the LCA (Fox & Farrington, 2012). Opportunistic burglaries were characterized by a lack of premeditation, as most offenses had unlawful (i.e., not forced) entry, meaning that a door, window, or garage was left open, allowing the burglar to enter without force. No tools were brought to the scene or used by the burglars, and these style burglaries typically occurred in unoccupied residential dwellings. Very low-value items were stolen (things that may be of interest to the burglar and not actually fenced or sold for money or drugs), and little evidence is generally left behind. They are crimes of opportunity.

Finally, interpersonal style burglaries, the least common of the four offense styles, were highly unique in that the victim of the burglary – not his or her possessions – were clearly the target of the crime. Unlike all other style burglaries, the interpersonal offenses typically occurred in occupied residential dwellings at nighttime and were often motivated by anger or dispute. In many cases, the offender attempted, threatened, or committed violence at the scene. These were highly confrontational offenses, which is unusual for a property crime such as burglary. In many ways, the interpersonal burglar appears to be a "wolf in sheep's clothing" and may be testing the waters for a more serious offense such as sexual battery, domestic violence, or homicide; many rapists and serial killers have burglary in their backgrounds (Schlesinger & Revitch, 1999).

Additional analyses revealed that these offense styles each tend to be committed by burglars with a unique set of traits and criminal histories. And in each case, the offending history and personality features of the criminal generally reflect the key behavioral features witnessed at the crime scene. Specifically, organized style burglaries tended to be committed by older offenders with a longer criminal history consisting of arrests for theft and burglary. These burglars tended to use manipulation and schemes to gain access to a property prior to the burglary (e.g., posing as a salesmen or a utility worker to see inside and "case" a residence) or have a job that they would use to facilitate burglary (e.g., tree trimming, construction, plumbing, electrician). In many cases the victim had met the offender, though the victim may not have known him or her very well. There would often be two or more organized burglars committing the crime to increase the amount of "loot" able to be stolen. For the same reason, organized burglars often had a car, which allowed a quick getaway to a location farther away from the victimized target.

Disorganized burglars tend to be young offenders with an early onset of criminal behavior. They are more versatile, with arrests for various crimes, including drugs. They often do not know the victim and select the target at random without premeditation or "casing" the location. They may be "high" while committing the offense or looking for drugs or items to quickly fence to buy drugs. Disorganized burglars are less likely to have cars, to be employed, or to have stability in their lives.

Opportunistic burglars are also young but tend not to have committed many (or any) offenses in the past. It is also likely that they do not know the victim and did not premeditate their crime but tend selected the location based upon an opportunity being presented (e.g., a window or door being left open). Opportunistic burglars are mostly male, but they also include the highest proportion of female burglars. If the burglar has a criminal history, it tends to be for petty offenses such as shoplifting, petty theft, or other opportunistic burglaries. They tend not to have a car and may commit these burglaries while skipping school or while bored over the summer months. Finally, interpersonal burglars also tend to be adult aged and almost always know the victim. However, they usually offend alone and tend to select female victims. Unlike other types of burglars, they enjoy the thrill of being in an occupied dwelling with the victim and may "case" the location to ensure that the victim is inside. Interpersonal burglar often do not have a criminal record, but if they do, it tends to be for crimes that reflect a need for power/control such as stalking, domestic violence, battery, and voyeurism. Interpersonal burglars are at highest risk of escalating to more severe crimes in the future.

These statistically generated profiles appear to support the original "organized/disorganized" profiles developed using a clinical approach by the FBI's BSU in the late 1970s. For instance, the FBI's organized profile for homicide described a very planned, methodical, and "professional" offense that tended to be committed by older, more experienced, and sophisticated offenders (Hazelwood & Douglas, 1980), which aligns with Fox and Farrington's (2012) organized profile of burglars. More specifically, organized murderers were said to bring a weapon with them to the crime and take it away with them (often due to attachment to the weapon and to avoid leaving evidence behind). The organized crime scenes contained little evidence, as the murder was methodically completed and often committed for utilitarian or instrumental reasons (Hazelwood & Douglas, 1980). Similarly, organized burglars were found to bring a tool with them to the scene and take it away with them, to leave little evidence, and to conduct a more sophisticated style crime largely to gain money or other items of value (Fox & Farrington, 2012).

Conversely, disorganized murderers are impulsive and frenzied, suggest little planning and premeditation, and often leave evidence behind (Hazelwood & Douglas, 1980). These features were also found in the statistical burglary profiles, in which crime scenes were often ransacked, the burglars did not come prepared with a tool, and evidence was often left behind (Fox & Farrington, 2012). Both disorganized murderers and burglars tend to be younger in age and less experienced than their organized counterparts (Fox & Farrington, 2012; Hazelwood & Douglas, 1980).

Notably, two new types of burglary profiles were found: opportunistic and interpersonal style offenses. It is possible that these profiles may also exist for violent crimes such as homicide and sexual offenses, and replication using samples of these offenders is highly necessary. Furthermore, replication of these profiles with the inclusion of personality traits, background, and mental health status of the offenders would be very beneficial, as these features have been shown to strongly relate to the offense behaviors and may increase the validity of the resulting profiles (Douglas et al., 1992).

Finally, direct replication of the profiles using data from burglaries committed in new locations, such as across the United States, Europe, Asia, and other areas, would demonstrate the reliability of the profiles across different cultures, contexts, and crime environments. In short, more research and replication is needed, in accordance with the EBOP approach.

EBOP juvenile sex offender profile

In a replication of the EBOP methodology, Fox and DeLisi (2018) used LCA to identify sub-types of male and female juvenile sex offenders located in Florida. Specifically, 4,143 juvenile sex offenders referred to the Florida Department of Juvenile Justice and turned 18 between 2007 and 2012 were included in the dataset. Developmental, psychological, and criminogenic risk factors, found to be predictive of juvenile sex offending in prior research, were used as indicator measures in the LCA. These measures included the age of criminal onset, the number of prior felony arrests, the levels of impulsivity and empathy, the presence of depression and psychosis, and a prior history of sexual abuse (see Fox, 2017; Seto & Lalumiére, 2010). The results indicated that there were four sub-types of male juvenile sex offenders: (1) non-disordered, (2) impulsive-unempathetic, (3) early-onset chronic, and (4) victim offenders, and two types of female juvenile sex offenders: (1) non-disordered and (2) victim offenders (Fox & DeLisi, 2018).

The non-disordered sub-type was found for both male and female juvenile sex offenders. These youth are distinct in that they show low impulsivity, tend to have empathy for their victims, rarely have mental health issues or symptomology, and tend not to have been sexually abused in childhood. The non-disordered sub-type tended to have an adolescent (age 13 to 15) or late (age 16 or older) onset of criminal behavior, and nearly all had two or fewer felony arrests. By comparison, the victim offender sub-type, which was also found for both male and female juvenile sex offenders, was characterized by a very high rate of mental health issues, including depression and psychosis. Most notably, 66% of male offenders and 85% of female offenders experienced sexual abuse in childhood, and many had an adolescent or early (age 12 or younger) onset of criminal behavior.

Two additional sub-types were found to exist only among the male juvenile sex offenders. The impulsive-unempathetic group showed very low levels of depression, psychosis, and childhood sexual abuse, but these youth were highly impulsive, and most felt no empathy towards their victims. Most of these youth also had three or more felony arrests. Finally, the early-onset chronic sub-type of male juvenile sex offenders had the highest proportion of youths with an early age of criminal onset, and 87% had three or more felonies on record. However, despite these criminogenic risk factors, these youths showed low rates of mental health issues and child-hood trauma.

These sub-types are the first statistically generated profiles of juvenile sex offenders, and they indicate that, even when the most predictive risk factors are included in the analysis, there are still heterogeneous sub-types that exist within the data. In other words, the most predictive risk factors are not present among all sex offenders, therefore illustrating an additional benefit of the use of statistical classification analyses to better understand offenders, their behaviors, and the potential reasons for their offending. Additionally, this replication of the EBOP approach using juvenile sex offenders suggests that there is a sub-type of offenders who are highly impulsive (and likely opportunistic in their offenses), a group who has an early criminal onset and a high rate of criminal activity (similar to the disorganized offenders), and a group of non-disordered offenders who are likely acting out for instrumental reasons (similar to the organized offenders). This suggests that there may be some consistency across offenses in the features of various sub-types of offenders. See Table 4.4 for comparisons of the describe EBOP profiles.

These findings are important for criminological research but even more important for practitioners who seek to understand, treat, and prevent offending. Typically, we seek to identify the most common predictors of criminal behavior, which are the significant risk factors in our models, and then develop interventions and prevention strategies targeting these risk factors. However, given the fact that research in the field of offender profiling consistently indicates that there is substantial heterogeneity among offenders and offenses, it does not appear that a "one size fits all" approach will be effective in preventing or reducing criminal behavior. By understanding the distinct and important differences among offenders, including burglars, murderers, sex offenders, and others, we are able to develop more tailored and effective policing and treatment responses that are best suited to address the unique risk factors among offenders or help police to identify the unique types of offenders based upon the types of crimes that they commit.

EBOP experimental field evaluation

A major concern among law enforcement is the accuracy of any new policing tool. An inaccurate technique, even if developed with the best intentions, may have a significant negative impact on investigations if it is utilized before challenges are identified. Similar concerns arise in the court system, as all policing techniques, such as profiling and polygraphing, must reach a significant level of accuracy, through scientific and peer-reviewed

Table 4.4 Summary of evidence-based offender profiles

Study	Crime type	EBOP profiles and description
Fox and Farrington (2012)	Burglary	*Organized* ■ Premeditated offense where foresight and care were taken to reduce risks and increase gains. Tools often brought to scene, used to force entry to location. Little or no evidence left behind; high-value items stolen that often require fencing or stolen goods network. Professional crime. *Disorganized* ■ Spontaneous and haphazard offense with little effort or concern towards avoiding apprehension. Crime scene often ransacked; evidence often left behind. Low-value items stolen; residential and commercial targets. Crime of disarray. *Opportunistic* ■ Characterized by lack of premeditation. Most offenses had unlawful entry; no tools brought to the scene. Occurred at unoccupied residences. Low-value items stolen. Little evidence left behind. Crime of opportunity. *Interpersonal* ■ Victim is the target, not his or her objects. Almost always occur at occupied residential dwellings at nighttime, motivated by anger or dispute. Offender often attempted, threatened, or committed violence at scene. Confrontational crime.

(*Continued*)

Study	Crime type	EBOP profiles and description
Fox and DeLisi (2018)	Juvenile sex offenders	*Non-disordered* ■ Found among male and female juvenile sex offenders. Distinctive in that the youth show low impulsivity, tend to have empathy for their victims, rarely have mental health issues, and tend not to have been sexually abused in childhood. Tended to have an adolescent (age 13 to 15) or late (age 16 or older) onset of offending, and nearly all had two or less prior felony arrests. *Impulsive-unempathetic* ■ Highly impulsive male offenders. Most felt no empathy towards their victims. These youth showed very low levels of depression, psychosis, and childhood sexual abuse, but most had three or more prior felony arrests. *Early-onset chronic* ■ Male offenders with an early age of criminal onset and three or more prior felonies on record. However, these youth showed low rates of mental health issues and childhood trauma. *Victim offenders* ■ Also found for both male and female juvenile sex offenders. Characterized by a very high rate of mental health issues, including depression and psychosis. The vast majority of these youth experienced sexual abuse in childhood, and many had an adolescent or early (age 12 or younger) onset of criminal behavior.

research, before being admitted as evidence (see Daubert v. Merrell Dow Pharmaceuticals, 1993).

Consequently, the scientific testing of profiling would not only help to identify the implications of using profiles out in the field, but it could also help to improve profiling as an accurate and reliable policing tool. With sufficient testing, appropriate scientific methods, positive results, and general acceptance in the field, profiling could also meet the scientific and legal requirements to be entered as evidence in court for the first time since 2001 (see *State v. Stevens*, 2001).

Therefore, one goal of EBOP is to test the utility of the resulting evidence-based profiles in actual police investigations using experimental field evaluations. Unlike prior offender profiling evaluation studies, which used less sophisticated designs that limit internal and external validity, experimental field research is able to more accurately assess the impact of offender profiles when used by police in their open investigations. In the first field experiment conducted to evaluate the impact of offender profiling, Fox and Farrington (2015) measured the effects of the evidence-based offender profiles for burglary that they developed using LCA.

Next, they conducted a multi-agency field experiment, which involved the cooperation of several major police departments in Florida that were matched on several key criteria such as crime rate, location, population, and number of sworn officers. One department, called the treatment group, was selected to receive training on the profiles and how to implement them in their burglary investigations. The remaining police departments served as control groups in the experiment, and conducted their investigations as usual without any use or knowledge of the EBOP burglary profiles.

To measure the success of the statistical behavioral profiles for burglary when applied in the field, the number of burglaries cleared by arrest in each police jurisdiction in the periods before and after the burglary profiles was used as the outcome measure. This item was operationalized using semi-annual (i.e., every 6 months) burglary arrest rates for each agency participating in the study for both the pre- and post-test evaluations. All pretest measures, including current burglary arrest rates, burglary incidence rates, and prior arrest rates, were collected semi-annually for each participating agency from January 1, 2008, until December 31, 2011, when the experimental period began. The same post-test measures were collected for a one-year follow-up period, from January 1, 2012, to December 31, 2012, for each department participating in the experiment.

After observing each of the departments' burglary arrest rates for one year, an analysis of covariance was used to compare the arrest rates for the treatment group with the rates of the control groups. Results show that while the average burglary arrest rates for the treatment and control

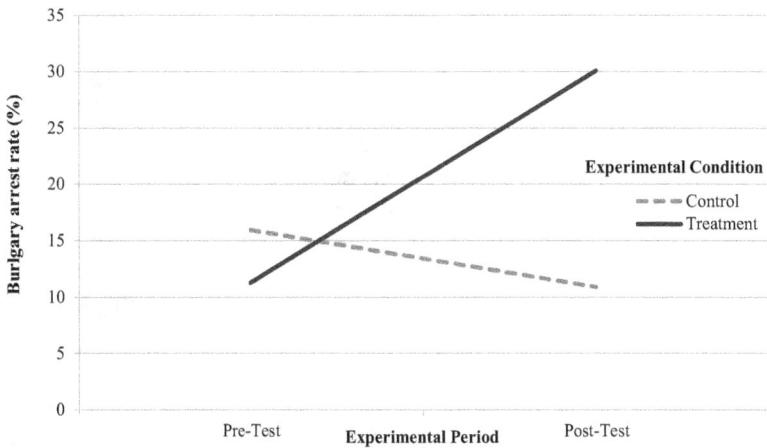

Figure 4.1 Evidence-Based Offender Profiles (Treatment) Effect on Burglary Arrest Rates.

agencies were initially very similar, the treatment agency actually started off slightly lower than the control agencies (11.3% vs. 15.9%, respectively). However, one year after the EBOP burglary profiles were implemented, the treatment agency had tripled its arrest rate from the pre-test to the post-test period, while the control arrest rate had slightly decreased (30.1% vs. 10.9%, respectively). This difference in the post-test burglary arrest rates for the treatment and control conditions yields a t-test odds ratio of 3.52 (95% confidence interval = [1.64, 7.52]), suggesting that the treatment agency was more than 3.5 times more likely to close an unsolved burglary than the agencies in the control condition after the EBOP burglary profiles were implemented. These results show that the EBOP burglary profiles can have a positive impact on the ability to solve cases, and this impact is quite substantial. See Figure 4.1 for a diagram of the experiment's results.

Conclusion

The goal of the evidence-based offender profiling approach is to develop new and effective tools for law enforcement that address problematic crimes using evidence-based methods and research. This approach specifies a scientific method to identify new offender profiles using large datasets and advanced statistical analyses, as well as an evaluation component which uses experimental designs to measure the effectiveness of EBOP profiles when implemented in actual police investigations. Initial research suggests that EBOP profiles can help to solve approximately three times more crimes as compared to standard police investigations, thereby demonstrating substantial benefits in terms of future crime prevention and cost savings to law enforcement. However, it is important to note that much more research needs to be conducted on the EBOP approach. For instance, it is integral to the EBOP methodology to replicate the profiles across different locations, cultures, law enforcement approaches, and time frames. This will help to determine the specific features of the EBOP profiles for each of the major regions within the United States and for nations across the globe, and then contrast consistencies and differences across these resulting profiles. Additionally, a randomized experiment would be useful to establish true causality between offender profiling and arrest rates, and examine how, and in what type of cases, profiles lead to an increased arrest rate. Such research would shed more light on the accuracy of the profiles, and indicate how to improve the profiles to better serve police and better solve open cases. We strongly encourage collaborations between law enforcement and academics on research such as this in the future.

In short, this chapter aimed to provide a clear overview of the EBOP approach as a stepping stone on the path to advancing the field of offender profiling and to apply this promising tool to address the most prolific and difficult-to-solve crimes across the globe.

References

Alison, L. J., Smith, M. D., & Morgan, K. (2003). Interpreting the accuracy of offender profiles. *Psychology, Crime & Law*, *9*, 185–195.

Bennell, C., & Canter, D. (2002). Linking commercial burglaries by modus operandi: Tests using regression and ROC analysis. *Science & Justice*, *42*, 153–164.

Bennell, C., Mugford, R., Ellingwood, H., & Woodhams, J. (2014). Linking crimes using behavioural clues: Current levels of linking accuracy and strategies for moving forward. *Journal of Investigative Psychology and Offender Profiling*, *11*, 29–56.

Campbell, C. (1976). Portrait of a mass killer. *Psychology Today*, *9*, 110–119.

Canter, D. V. (1995). Psychology of offender profiling. In R. Bull & D. Carson (Eds.), *Handbook of psychology in legal contexts* (pp. 343–355). New York, NY: John Wiley & Sons.

Copson, G. (1995). *Coals to Newcastle? Part 1: A study of offender profiling.* London: Home Office, Police Research Group.

Daubert v. Merrell Dow Pharmaceuticals, Inc. (1993). 113 S.Ct. 2786.

Douglas, J. E., Burgess, A. W., Burgess, A. G., & Ressler, R. K. (1992). *Crime classification manual.* New York, NY: Lexington Books.

Douglas, J. E., Ressler, R. K., Burgess, A. W., & Hartman, C. R. (1986). Criminal profiling from crime scene analysis. *Behavioral Sciences and the Law*, *4*, 401–421.

Dowden, C., Bennell, C., & Bloomfield, S. (2007). Advances in offender profiling: A systematic review of the profiling literature published over the past three decades. *Journal of Police and Criminal Psychology, 22*, 44–56.

Farrington, D. P., & Lambert, S. (2000). Statistical approaches to offender profiling. In D. V. Canter & L. J. Alison (Eds.), *Profiling property crimes* (pp. 233–274). Aldershot: Ashgate Publishing.

Farrington, D. P., Snyder, H. N., & Finnegan, T. A. (1988). Specialization in juvenile court careers. *Criminology, 3*, 461–487.

Farrington, D. P., & Welsh, B. C. (2006). A half century of randomized experiments on crime and justice. *Crime and Justice, 34*, 55–132.

Fox, B. (2017). What makes a difference? Evaluating the key distinctions and predictors of sexual and nonsexual offending among male and female juvenile offenders. *Journal of Criminal Psychology, 7*(2), 134–150.

Fox, B., & DeLisi, M. (2018). From criminological heterogeneity to coherent classes: Developing a typology of juvenile sex offenders. *Youth Violence and Juvenile Justice, 16*(3), 299–318.

Fox, B., & Farrington, D. P. (2012). Creating burglary profiles using latent class analysis: A new approach to offender profiling. *Criminal Justice and Behavior, 39*, 1582–1611.

Fox, B., & Farrington, D. P. (2015). An experimental evaluation of the utility of burglary profiles applied in active police investigations. *Criminal Justice and Behavior, 42*, 156–175.

Fox, B., & Farrington, D. P. (2018). What have we learned from offender profiling? A systematic review and meta-analysis of 40 years of research. *Psychological Bulletin, 144*, 1247–1274.

Francis, B., Bowater, R., & Soothill, K. (2004). *Using homicide data to assist murder investigations* (Home Office online report). London: Home Office.

Geberth, V. J. (1990). Serial killer and the revelation of Ted Bundy. *Law and Order, 38*, 72–77.

Gudjonsson, G. H., & Copson, G. (1997). The role of the expert in criminal investigations. In J. L. Jackson & D. A. Bekerian (Eds.), *Offender profiling: Theory, research and practice* (pp. 1–7). New York, NY: John Wiley & Sons.

Hazelwood, R. R., & Burgess, A. W. (Eds.). (1987). *Practical aspects of rape investigation: A multidisciplinary approach.* New York, NY: Elsevier.

Hazelwood, R. R., & Douglas, J. (1980). The lust murderer. *FBI Law Enforcement Journal, 49*, 18–22.

Holmes, R. M., & Holmes, S. T. (1996). *Profiling violent crimes: An investigative tool.* Thousand Oaks, CA: Sage.

Jackson, J. L., van Koppen, P. J., & Herbrink, J. C. M. (1993). *Does the service meet the needs?* (Report NSCR WD94-03). Leiden: Netherlands Institute for the Study of Criminality and Law Enforcement (NISCALE).

Jeffers, H. P. (1991). *Who killed precious? How FBI special agents combine psychology and high technology to identify violent criminals.* New York, NY: Pharos Books.

Kocsis, R. N. (Ed.). (2007). *Criminal profiling: International theory, research, and practice.* Totowa, NJ: Humana Press.

Kocsis, R. N., & Cooksey, R. W. (2002). Criminal psychological profiling of serial arson crimes. *International Journal of Offender Therapy and Comparative Criminology*, *46*, 631–656.

Kocsis, R. N., & Hayes, A. F. (2004). Believing is seeing? Investigating the perceived accuracy of criminal psychological profiles. *International Journal of Offender Therapy and Comparative Criminology*, *48*, 149–160.

Kocsis, R. N., & Heller, G. Z. (2004). Believing is seeing-II: Beliefs and perceptions of criminal psychological profiles. *International Journal of Offender Therapy and Comparative Criminology*, *48*, 313–329.

Kocsis, R. N., & Middledorp, J. T. (2004). Believing is seeing III: Perceptions of content in criminal psychological profiles. *International Journal of Offender Therapy and Comparative Criminology*, *48*, 477–494.

Kocsis, R. N., & Palermo, G. B. (2007). Critiques and conceptual dimensions to criminal profiling. In R. N. Kocsis (Ed.), *Criminal profiling: International theory, research, and practice* (pp. 327–345). Totowa, NJ: Humana Press.

Lösel, F. (2008). Doing evaluation research in criminology: Balancing scientific and practical demands. In R. King & E. Wincup (Eds.), *Doing research on crime and justice* (2nd ed., pp. 141–170). New York, NY: Oxford University Press.

Muthen, L. K., & Muthen, B. O. (2000). *Mplus user's guide* (5th ed.). Los Angeles, CA: Muthen & Muthen.

Pinizzotto, A. J. (1984). Forensic psychology: Criminal personality profiling. *Journal of Police Science and Administration*, *12*, 32–40.

Ressler, R. K., Burgess, A. W., & Douglas, J. E. (1988). *Sexual homicide: Patterns and motives*. Lexington, MA: Lexington Books.

Rossmo, D. K. (1999). *Geographic profiling*. Boca Raton, FL: CRC Press.

Schlesinger, L. B., & Revitch, E. (1999). Sexual burglaries and sexual homicides: Clinical, forensic, and investigative considerations. *Journal of the American Academy of Psychiatry and Law*, *27*, 227–238.

Seto, M. C., & Lalumiére, M. L. (2010). What is so special about male adolescent sex offending? A review and test of explanations through meta-analysis. *Psychological Bulletin*, *136*, 526–575.

Snook, B., Taylor, P. J., & Bennell, C. (2007). Criminal profiling belief and use: A study of Canadian police officer opinion. *Canadian Journal of Police and Security Services*, *5*, 1–11.

Snook, B., Taylor, P. J., Gendreau, P., & Bennell, C. (2009). On the need for scientific experimentation in the criminal profiling field: A reply to Dern and colleagues. *Criminal Justice and Behavior*, *36*, 1091–1094.

State v. Stevens. (2001). Tennessee 78 S.W. 817.

Steadman, H. J., Silver, E., Monahan, J., Appelbaum, P. S., Robbins, P. C., Mulvey, E. P., . . . Banks, S. (2000). A classification tree approach to the development of actuarial violence risk assessment tools. *Law and Human Behavior*, *24*, 83–100.

Swets, J. A. (1988). Measuring the accuracy of diagnostic systems. *Science*, *240*, 1285–1293.

Trager, J., & Brewster, J. (2001). The effectiveness of psychological profiles. *Journal of Police and Criminal Psychology*, *16*, 20–28.

Uebersax, J. (2009). *Latent class analysis: Frequently asked questions. Latent structure analysis*. Retrieved from www.john-uebersax.com/stat/index.htm.

US House of Representatives. (1990, March 5). *U.S.S. Iowa tragedy: An investigative failure* (Report of the investigations subcommittee and the defense policy panel of the committee on armed services). Washington, DC: US House of Representatives 101st Congress, 2nd Session.

Vermunt, J. K., & Magidson, J. (2005). *Latent gold 4.0 user's guide*. Boston, MA: Statistical Innovations.

5 International replication of evidence-based offender profiles in the United Kingdom[1]

Introduction

Differences in criminal experience have been found to influence the way an offender behaves when committing an offense. Mawby (2001) suggested that most burglaries are planned, rational acts and that unplanned, opportunistic styles are rarely represented. Although this may be evident in many cases, research has consistently identified distinct groups of burglary styles. Maguire and Bennett (1982) highlight the disagreement among researchers for the best term to use in describing a so-called "professional burglar". They suggest that domestic burglars can fall into one of three categories: low-level amateurs, mid-level professionals, and high-level professionals. This finding of distinct sub-groups of burglars is reflective of the literature suggesting that burglary tends to be a more professional offense, albeit with differing expertise and behavior among offenders. Although not developed as a uniform classification of burglars, similarities to this seminal work are noted throughout the literature.

As discussed in Chapter 4, Fox and Farrington (2012) examined co-occurring features of crimes, producing profiles that consider behavioral variations between offenders. They identified several categories of offense actions, offender traits, and criminal history, yielding four profiles of burglary: opportunistic, organized, disorganized, and interpersonal. The present chapter draws cross-cultural comparisons of the US and UK burglary profiles.

The scientific method of drawing inferences on offender characteristics from offending actions is summarized by Canter (1995) as the A (actions) to C (characteristics) equation, also known as the "profiling equation". This approach is based on the premise of co-occurring behavioral features of a crime (e.g., time of day, method of operation) being statistically related to offender characteristics (e.g., criminal history, age, race, sex). The challenges faced in understanding actions and characteristics is that they will rarely take one form. Canter and Youngs (2009) state that the relationship between actions and characteristics is canonical, whereby the relationship is not one to one but a combination of the two mapping spaces onto each other. Thus, a multivariate approach is needed to analyze these sorts of relationships. It is hypothesized that, when analyzing burglars, there will not be distinct "types" of burglars or burglaries, but themes of distinct and overlapping offense and offender characteristics. Although an individual can sit within a themed region of behavioral style, it does not mean that they cannot move between these styles. As Maguire and Bennett (1982) state, it is important to understand the systems of behaviors and the reasons behind them rather than to "type" each offender based on her or his offending characteristics. Furthermore, it is important to replicate prior research on the association between specific types of behaviors and types of offenders, to determine if these subtypes and relationships are generalizable to offenders across time and place.

Data collection and content analysis

The aim of this study was to statistically analyze the association between crime scene behaviors of burglary and features of the offenders. It was hypothesized that inferences on the characteristics of burglars can be derived based on offender criminal history, demographic traits, and offense behavioral style.

Police recorded data from a major metropolitan city in England and data from the Police National Computer (PNC) were used in the analysis of the offenses and offender criminal histories. The dataset consisted of 1,017 offender–offense cases of convicted burglaries committed between 2011 and 2015. The analysis focuses on a sample of domestic and commercial burglaries to identify any distinctions between the two. It was essential to use solved cases to assess the offender's background, as the unsolved sample will not have valid reference to an offender.

Variables based on the offender's criminal history, traits, and offense style were obtained. Table 5.1 displays a breakdown of the frequencies for these variables. To make comparisons to other findings on profiling burglary, the current study used a similar coding dictionary to Fox and Farrington (2012).

Criminal history

Burglary and theft occur in over 90% of the sample's previous history. The most common crimes in the sample's history include violence (71%), drugs (75%), criminal damage (65%), and shoplifting (53%). The time span in years of offending and total number of prior offenses gives an indication of the degree of offending experience, prior to the burglary being analyzed. Offenders within the sample display extensive criminal experience with 65% offending for 6 to 30 years, whilst 91% have had 3 or more prior

Table 5.1 Descriptive statistics for all burglary offender and offense characteristics

Criminal history

Item	Frequency	Percent	Item	Frequency	Percent
0 years offending	19	2	Previous burglary	975	96
1–5 years offending	283	28	Previous theft	942	93
6–30 years offending g	660	65	Previous violence	717	71
30+ years offending	55	5	Previous drugs	679	67
No prior offenses	28	3	Previous criminal damage	657	65
1–2 prior offences	59	6	Previous shoplifting	534	53
3+ prior offenses	930	91	Previous driving offense	486	48
Early onset	746	73	Previous firearms	161	16
Adolescent onset	236	23	Previous fraud	108	11
Late onset	35	3	Previous rape	78	8
Network association	518	51	Previous arson	77	8
Previous co-offense	747	73	Previous sexual offense	75	7
Offender knew victim	54	5	Previous murder	28	3
			Previous indecent assault	10	1

Offender characteristics

Item	Frequency	Percent	Item	Frequency	Percent
White	748	74	Brown eyes	456	45
Black	170	17	Green eyes	12	1
Asian	31	3	Blue eyes	348	34
Offender male	948	93	Offender short	211	21
Offender female	67	7	Offender average	709	70

Offender characteristics

Item	Frequency	Percent	Item	Frequency	Percent
Offender adolescent	154	15	Offender tall	36	4
Offender young adult	487	48	Offender unemployed	533	52
Offender adult	376	37	Offender student	29	3
Brown hair	489	48	Offender school child	24	2
Black hair	228	22	5% deprivation	257	25
Blonde hair	88	9	10% deprivation	126	12
Other hair colour	212	21	20% deprivation	146	14
			30% deprivation	46	5

Offense characteristics

Item	Frequency	Percent	Item	Frequency	Percent
Commercial burglary	298	29	Exit same as entry	420	41
Residential burglary	710	70	MO smash	255	25
Daytime offense	481	47	MO insecure	298	29
Night-time offense	536	53	MO unlock	130	13
Entry front	235	23	MO force lock	55	5
Entry window	450	44	MO climb	96	9
Entry rear	451	44	MO force	248	24
Entry door	412	41	Weapon key	152	15
Entry side	70	7	Weapon foot	48	5
Exit front	186	18	Weapon unknown	246	24
Exit window	187	18	Alarm fitted	138	14
Exit rear	358	35	Credit card	67	7
Exit door	400	39	High value stolen	205	20
Exit side	46	5	Low value stolen	812	80

Note: Percentages calculated excluding missing values.

offenses. As with Fox and Farrington's study, the age of onset was calculated by subtracting the offender's date of birth from the date of the last
offense. Based upon the developmental and life-course literature, age of
onset was coded into three groups: early onset (7 to 14 years old), adolescent onset (15 to 20 years old), and late onset (21 years and over). Early-
onset offenders have previously been shown to be more diverse in their
offending history (e.g., Farrington et al., 2006, 2013). About 73% of the
sample is early onset, adding further support to the offenders within the
sample being highly experienced.

Offender characteristics

The age of offenders within the sample ranged from 12 to 63 years old, with
a mean age of 26 (standard deviation = 9.74). The age of the offenders was
coded as adolescent (11 to 17 years old), young adult (18 to 24 years old)
or adult (25 years old and older). Nearly half of the offenders (48%) were
young adults at the time of the present offense, 37% were adults, and 15%
were adolescents. The age of the offender is important in understanding his
or her stage of psychological and criminal development.

The English Indices of Deprivation (IMD) for 2010 provide a level of
deprivation in each small area of land across the United Kingdom. Each
area is assessed for levels of income, employment, health and disability,
barriers to housing or services, crime, and living environment, and a com-
bined overall level of depression and then placed into a nationwide rank
order. Rank orders are then divided into percentages, which then provide
an indication as to the relative levels of deprivation in an area (Table 5.2).
Although not previously analyzed in a study of this kind, the level of
deprivation was assessed to see whether there were differences between

Table 5.2 Deprivation percentage score categories

Rank order	Percentage category
1–325	1% *(most deprived)*
326–1,824	5%
1,825–3,248	10%
3,249–6,496	20%
6,497–9,744	30%
9,745–12,002	40%
12,003–16,240	50%
16,241–19,488	60%
19,489–22,736	70%
22,737–32,472	71%–100% *(least deprived)*

offenders from different areas. Levels of deprivation within the sample were shown to range between 5% and 30% across offenders.

Offense characteristics

After coding the location and time of the offenses, a higher percentage of residential versus commercial burglaries was found, and an almost equal split between daytime and nighttime offenses. The most common entry methods were entry through the window (44%), rear (44%), and door (41%), while entering through the front (23%) and to the side (7%) did not occur as often. Method of exit showed that the offenders were exiting in the way that they entered, with a high frequency of exit rear (35%) and door (39%).

The most frequent crime scene behaviors were offenders targeting an insecure property (i.e. unlawful entry) (29%), smashing to gain entry (25%), and use of force to gain entry (24%). Property stolen was coded based on whether it was a high- (>£300) or low-value (<=£300) loss. Only 20% of the sample stole high-value items, while 80% stole low value items, indicating varying offender motivations in terms of gain and thrill-seeking. Only 14% of the burglaries had an alarm on the property. In their study on a burglar's decision to offend, Bennett and Wright (1984) found that nearly half of the interviewed offenders reported that an alarm deterred them. These offenders also noted that in some cases, they were willing to take the risk where a larger reward would be gained. On the other hand, Bennett and Wright (1984) also identified burglars who were not deterred from entering a home with an alarm because they could escape quickly if the alarm went off.

Analysis

Two-step cluster analysis was used in identifying sub-types of criminal history, offender characteristics, and offense styles. The aim was to identify behavioral clusters that highlight styles of offending behavior and distinctions between previous criminal experience and offender characteristics. Smallest space analysis (SSA) was then used to derive relationships between the characteristics and the offender details. This method allows for the co-occurrence of each of the characteristics of criminal history, offense behaviors, and offender traits to be measured against each other and presented via graphical representation of the variables.

Two-step cluster analysis is particularly useful in exploring a database with the aim of deriving groups, or clusters, that are not otherwise obvious. This procedure will compare the values of a model-choice criterion, in this case Bayesian information criterion (BIC), across different clustering solutions. Chi-square tests were conducted to assess any statistical relationships within the clusters and to determine if the relationships were significantly different from chance. Adjusted standardized residual (ASR) tests were also conducted to measure the strength of the difference between observed and expected values in cells. As in Fox and Farrington's (2012) study, the ASR is used in considering the overall size of the sample and gives the best indication of differences between the observed and expected values. A general rule for ASR values is that if the residual is less than -1.96, the cell's observed frequency is less than the expected frequency (at $p<.05$, two-tailed), and if the residual is greater than 1.96, then the observed frequency is significantly greater than the expected frequency.

Although recent studies have used latent class analysis (LCA) for finding sub-types of related cases, two-step cluster analysis is closely related to it. Both methods are used to quantitatively discover groups or types of cases based on observed data and possibly to also assign cases to groups. Early studies have successfully used cluster analysis to study patterns of groups within data. For example, Green, Booth, and Biderman (1976) used cluster analysis to derive sub-types of burglary methods of operation. More recently, Ennis, Buro, and Jung (2016) applied cluster analysis to a sample of male sexual offenders, highlighting three sub-types based on low, moderate, and high risk groups.

Although the two analyses work on similar principles, the SSA items are not confined to a linear space, and fewer assumptions are made about the underlying structure of the variables. Instead this method allows the relationship of every variable to every other variable to be represented in a three-dimensional space. If variables co-occur, then they will be positioned closer together in the space. The final plot will display thematic regions in relation to each of the items that co-occur. The main issue with cluster analysis is in determining the criterion cut-off point of whether something will cluster or not, which can be problematic. The arbitrariness of putting items into a group or not means that you do not get the boundary conditions that are defined with SSA regional interpretations. The cluster analysis, in this case, will be used to focus on the variables that are distinct from the rest to then validate using SSA. By cross-validating the regional themes of the SSA, a clearer representation of differing styles of burglary can be presented.

Resulting profiles

Two-step cluster analysis

The cluster analysis displayed reasonable quality clusters based on the measure of cohesion and separation for criminal history types (average silhouette = 0.30, ratio sizes = 2.10), offender traits (average silhouette = 0.30, ratio sizes = 1.88), and offense characteristics (average silhouette = 0.20, ratio sizes = 3.25).

Criminal history is defined by the number of previous offenses and the total years of offending. The cluster analysis indicates an offending time span of 1 to 5 years and 6 to 30 years as highly important predictors. High-rate (HR) offenders (68%) have more criminal convictions, indicating greater experience committing offenses. Along with violence (48%) and drugs (42%) offenses, the low-rate (LR) offenders (32%) also have a high percentage of shoplifting offenses (46%), indicative of the inexperienced nature of the LR offenders.

The race and hair color of the offenders are the most predictive features for cluster distinction when examining the offender traits, resulting in three cluster labels. The first cluster, labelled Adult Minority Male (AMM), occurring in 24% of the sample, displays the highest percentage of black (67%) and Asian (12%) offenders. The second cluster labelled the Younger White Male (YWM), occurring in 31%, are predominantly white (79%) males (90%), with the highest percentage of adolescent offenders (31%). The Adult White Male (AWM), occurring in 45% of the sample, contains the highest percentage of white (99%) male (96%) offenders. The demographics of the area, as well as the dataset, are mostly white individuals. Unsurprisingly, the highest frequency of offenders is within the AWM cluster.

Analysis of offense characteristics resulted in four clusters. The burglary type and the time of day were the most predictive features for differentiation across offenses. The purely commercial offending style, labelled Non-Domestic (ND), comprised 25% of the sample, and contains many different offense characteristics. The second offending style, labelled Forceful, comprised 10% of the sample, and display high frequency of force (32%) in comparison with the other offending styles. Two clusters relate solely to domestic burglary, suggesting that domestic burglars will differ more in the method of operation than ND burglars. These offending styles are almost identical, except one occurs only at night against mainly insecure properties, labelled Interpersonal, occurring in 32% of the sample. The other, in 33% of the sample, occurs during the day, involves stealing high value goods, and displays evidence of using a weapon, labelled Skilled-Domestic (SD).

The results indicate statistically significant relationships between the three offender trait clusters (AMM, AWM, and YWM) and the four offense characteristic (ND, Forceful, Interpersonal, and SD) clusters ($\chi^2 = 26.30$, df = 6, $p<.001$). The relationship between the AMM and the Interpersonal cluster produced a positive statistically significant ASR value (ASR = 3.5, $p<.05$).

This indicates substantially more AMM offenders offend in an interpersonal style than predicted by chance. A significant, but negative, ASR value is found between the AMM and ND clusters. This means that there are fewer ND burglaries committed by AMM offenders than expected (ASR = –3.4, p<.05). A positive significant ASR value indicated that more ND burglaries are committed by YWM than expected by chance (ASR = 3.6, p<.05). A significant negative ASR value was found between the YWM and Interpersonal offending style (ASR = –3.6, p<.05), indicating that less inexperienced offenders committed this style.

The relationship between the AWM and the offending styles did not indicate any significant strength based on the ASR values. However, 36% of AWM are associated to the SD burglary offending style. No statistically significant relationship was identified for the Forceful burglar.

Chi-square tests also indicated significant relationships between the three offender trait (AMM, AWM, and YWM) and the two criminal history (HR and LR) clusters (χ^2 = 47.63, df = 2, p<.001). The YWM were significantly related to the LR criminal history cluster, highlighting their lack of criminal experience. A positive significant ASR value indicates that more YWM have a LR of criminal experience than expected by chance (ASR = 6.7, p<.05). The HR criminal history type showed a statistical association to the AWM. This coincides with the relationship highlighted between offender traits and offense characteristics, whereby the AWM are shown to relate to the SD type of burglary. The positive significant ASR value indicates that offenders who commit the SD offending style tend to be more criminally experienced (ASR = 5.5, p<.05). The AMM did not show a significant relationship to either the high- or low-rate criminal history type. However, this offender trait cluster did occur more in the HR criminal history cluster, showing that the AMM had a similar criminal background to the AWM.

There was no significant association identified between the offense characteristic and criminal history clusters. This finding was also observed in Fox and Farrington's (2012) study, in which a general relationship between offense style and criminal history type was not significant.

Smallest space analysis

The central principle in interpreting the SSA plot is referred to as the "regional hypothesis". Co-occurring behaviors are positioned closer in the multidimensional space, forming regions of items that share a commonality. However, not all items share the same meaning. Any slight change in the variables, and based on how the resulting configuration is interpreted, could change their positioning in a different region of the plot. The item frequencies are an important aspect in identifying patterns of relationships between variables. The behaviors on the outside of the plot are more specific behaviors providing a qualitative variation. In contrast, behaviors in the center of the plot share common features and thus group together centrally. Behaviors that were either very high or low frequency were removed from the SSA analysis because they could distort the findings.

Initial examination of the variables within the plot displayed a mixture of offense, offender, and criminal history characteristics, showing that there is a relationship between the characteristics and the offense details. The chi-square analysis of the different clusters gives an indication as to which behaviors will co-occur. For example, the Interpersonal offending style and the AMM were shown to be statistically significant. We would therefore expect to see the "black" offender variable situated close to "MO insecure".

The final SSA solution is presented in Figure 5.1, displaying four themed regions that develop from the core of the plot. The three-dimensional resulting configuration has a coefficient of alienation of 0.23 with 14 iterations, indicating a good fit of the co-occurrences of listed characteristics. The regions are labelled based on offending styles identified in the cluster analysis: SD, Forceful, Interpersonal, and ND.

The results indicate that the cluster analysis can be mapped onto the SSA with a bit of overlap, indicating the difficulty of placing a group of burglaries into specific types or clusters. Instead, there are defined regions of offending behaviors relating to an offender's traits and previous criminal history.

Types of UK burglaries versus types of UK burglars

Skilled-Domestic

The SD region in Figure 5.1 displays behaviors that portray a burglary committed by an offender with previous experience, likely in the prime of their offending. These actions include the burglary being residential (70%), daytime (47%), rear entry (44%), window entry (44%), smashing (25%), use of a weapon (24%), and climbing (9%). The offender traits and criminal histories within this region include previous violence (71%), 6 to 30 years of offending experience (65%), offender unemployed (52%), criminal network association (51%), offender young adult (48%), offender home within 5% deprivation level (25%), and previous firearms offense (16%).

Although the SD style indicates an offender who knows what he or she is doing, this does not necessarily mean that the offender will be the most experienced. A Kendall's tau-b correlation was run to determine the

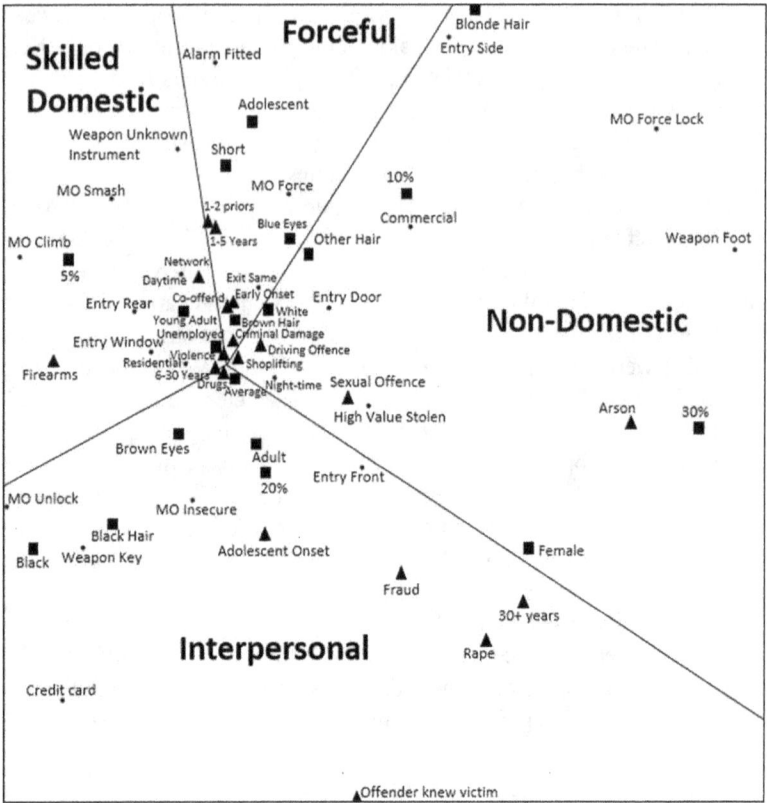

Figure 5.1 One-by-two projection of the three-dimensional SSA-I

Note: circle = offense actions, square = offender characteristics, triangle = criminal history.

relationship between the SD burglary style and the age, total convictions, and years active of the offenders. There was a weak negative correlation with offender age, which was statistically significant ($\tau b = -.086$, $p<.01$). This suggests that offenders committing burglaries in this style tend to be younger in age. A non-significant positive relationship was found for total convictions and a non-significant negative relationship for years active.

Forceful

The offending actions found to be positioned within this region are exit the same way entered (41%), force (24%), and alarm fitted at the property (14%). Properties in which an alarm is fitted included in the offending styles but is shown to be positioned within the Forceful theme. However, 36% of burglaries where the property is fitted with an alarm were committed by an SD burglar, while 28% were Forceful burglars. The difference between the two is likely in the offender's criminal experience. The SD burglar may have experience in dismantling alarms. Since the Forceful offender tends to be younger in age, he or she may be scared off by the alarm. The nature of this offending style indicates offenders who take little care in the offense, leading to their detection during the act. Previous studies found that when an offender is noticed and disturbed, she or he will flee the scene, leading to unsuccessful attempts (Paine, 2012; Robb, Coupe, & Ariel, 2015). The low occurrence of this offending style indicates that a Forceful burglary is likely to be conducted by someone less experienced, acting on a trial-and-error basis.

The offender characteristics positioned within this region imply that these burglaries may also be carried out for fun and excitement, such as by younger offenders. This is shown through the offender traits and criminal histories positioned in this region: previous co-offending (73%), early onset (73%), brown hair (48%), previous criminal damage (65%), blue eyes (34%), one to five years offending experience (28%), short in height (21%), offender adolescent (15%), and having one or two prior offenses (6%).

Negative significant correlations were found between the Forceful offending style and age ($\tau b = -.370$, $p<.01$), total convictions ($\tau b = -.105$, $p<.01$), and years active ($\tau b = -.263$, $p<.01$). This suggests an association between this offending style and younger offenders within the sample, with a low number of prior convictions and less criminal experience.

Interpersonal

The offense actions displayed within this region are burglaries against insecure properties (29%), front entry (23%), weapon key (15%), and credit card stolen (7%). Although offenses occurring at nighttime are situated within the ND region, the cluster analysis indicated all the Interpersonal burglaries occurred at night. This behavior is positioned close to the Interpersonal theme, bordering the ND, demonstrating a degree of overlap of offense actions across styles.

Inferences can be made about the offender character based on the traits and criminal history identified within this region. These are: previous drug (67%), rape (8%), and fraud (11%) offenses, brown eyes (45%), adult offender (37%), adolescent onset (23%), black hair (17%), black offender (17%), comes from a 20% level of deprivation area (14%), 30 or more years of offending (5%), and knowing the victim (5%). The regional divide suggests that the Interpersonal style will be committed by offenders who are older, and therefore likely to have more criminal experience. This is supported by positive significant correlations shown between the offender's age (τb = .393, *p*<.01), total convictions (τb = .286, *p*<.01), and years active (τb = .355, *p*<.01) and the Interpersonal behavioral style.

Non-Domestic

The main distinguishing feature of this region in comparison to the others is that these offenses are conducted on commercial properties rather than residential ones. The offense actions found within this region include: the offense occurring at night-time (53%), entry door (41%), commercial burglary (29%), high-value stolen (20%), entry side (7%), force lock (5%), and using foot as weapon (5%). A statistically significant relationship was found between the offense occurring at night-time and high-value items stolen (χ^2 1, n = 1017) = 11.910, *p*<.01). This means that offenses occurring during the nighttime may be more lucrative than those during the day.

The offender traits and previous offending history positioned within this region include the offender being white (74%), previous shoplifting (53%), and driving offenses (48%), coming from a 10% level of deprivation area (12%), blonde hair (9%), previous arson (8%), previous sexual offense (7%), and being female (7%). Correlations showed weak positive significant relationships between the ND behavioral style and the offender age (τb = .060, *p*<.01), total convictions (τb = .184, *p*<.01), and years active (τb = .105, *p*<.01). Although no strong correlation is shown, the findings do highlight that offenders displaying this offending style tend to be older, to have a higher number of convictions, and to have longer criminal careers.

Comparison of UK with US burglary profiles

The current study findings showed similarities to previous studies aiming to predict offender traits from offense actions. Fox and Farrington (2012) examined co-occurring features of burglaries in the United States, thus producing profiles that considered the behavioral variations between offenders. In their sample of 405 solved burglary cases, they identified several categories of offense actions, offender traits, and criminal history. The sub-types of these were shown to display four profiles of burglary, labelled opportunistic, organized, disorganized, and interpersonal.

In comparison, the UK Forceful offending style displays some similarities to the offense actions of the Floridian "disorganized" burglar. The similarities of these profiles relate to the offender's use of force and failed attempts in offending. However, Fox and Farrington highlighted their "disorganized" burglar as having a long criminal career, whereas the current findings show an analogous offender sub-type having very little criminal experience. The current findings suggest that, like the Floridian disorganized burglar, the

Forceful burglar will begin offending at a young age, and continue offending into adulthood.

The Interpersonal burglars in this study also display similarities to the Fox and Farrington burglary profiles. A key behavior displayed in the UK Interpersonal offending style is the property being insecure and in many cases occurring at nighttime (65%), with the likelihood of the properties being occupied increased. Similarly, Fox and Farrington's Floridian interpersonal offenders were shown to have low skill, but their offenses were mostly committed at night with a high personal involvement, targeting residential properties, and motivated by anger. A statistically significant relationship was identified between the property being insecure and the offender being black (χ^2 (1, n = 1017) = 12.551, p<.001). Although not statistically significant, the sample shows that almost 60% of the burglaries that occur at nighttime were carried out by black offenders. These findings coincide with Fox and Farrington's interpersonal offending style, which was found to have the strongest association with older black men.

Fox and Farrington's organized burglar displayed similar traits to the current study's SD burglar. In both studies, these offenders were shown to use more skill in their offenses and were likely to have brought a tool or weapon to the scene. Offender characteristics were also shown to be similar, with organized offenses mostly committed by the white male group.

Fox and Farrington (2012) did not identify a distinct offender who focuses solely on commercial properties. Given that the area sampled in their study covers 1,200 square miles of the east coast of Florida, whereas the current study is sampled from a roughly 30-square-mile major metropolitan city in the United Kingdom, there are surprising resemblances in the findings. Importantly, this study underscores the potential generalizability of offense-offender profiles among small-town American burglars and those of a dense major metropolitan city in the United Kingdom.

Conclusion

The current study successfully identifies a new model of burglary differentiation, labelled SD, Forceful, Interpersonal, and ND. These findings provide important implications in understanding the psychological differences between burglaries and in understanding offenders' natural tendency to change behaviors according to their environment.

By establishing a scientific model of domestic burglary based on observable behavioral data, the findings have direct policy implications for police investigations. This includes relevant investigative information for unsolved offenses that allows for insights about the unknown offender.

A crucial component of this study was the further replication of the American evidence-based offender profiles for burglary, by grouping offense actions with characteristics of offenders. Use of a the thematic approach to studying offending styles, in considering themes along which crimes can be differentiated, displays a realistic approach to dynamic human nature. Specifically, MDS techniques allow for the interpretation of broader themes in offense and offender characteristics, rather than placing an individual into one conceptual box (especially when overlap across offense/offender profiles is common). Future research would benefit from further exploration of the use of MDS procedures in classifying patterns of burglary, and further efforts to replicate evidence-based offender profiles across different nations.

Note

1 The assistance of Donna Youngs and David V. Canter with the project described in this chapter is gratefully acknowledged.

References

Bennett, T., & Wright, R. (1984). *Burglars on burglary: Prevention and the offender*. Aldershot: Gower.

Canter, D. (1995). Psychology of offender profiling. In R. Bull & D. Carson (Eds.), *Handbook of psychology in legal contexts* (pp. 343–355). Chichester: John Wiley & Sons.

Canter, D., & Youngs, D. (2009). *Investigative psychology: Offender profiling and the analysis of criminal action*. Chichester: John Wiley & Sons.

Ennis, L., Buro, K., & Jung, S. (2016). Identifying male sexual offender subtypes using cluster analysis and the static-2002R. *Sexual Abuse, 28*(5), 403–426.

Farrington, D. P., Coid, J. W., Harnett, L., Jolliffe, D., Soteriou, N., Turner, R., & West, D. J. (2006). Criminal Careers up to age 50 and Life Success up to age 48: New Findings from the Cambridge Study in Delinquent Development. (Research Study No. 299). London: Home Office.

Farrington, D. P., Piquero, A. R., & Jennings, W. G. (2013). Offending from Childhood to Late Middle Age: Recent Results from the Cambridge Study in Delinquent Development. New York, NY: Springer.

Fox, B., & Farrington, D. P. (2012). Creating burglary profiles using latent class analysis: A new approach to offender profiling. *Criminal Justice and Behavior, 39*(12), 1582–1611.

Green, E. J., Booth, C. E., & Biderman, M. D. (1976). Cluster analysis of burglary M/Os. *Journal of Police Science and Administration, 4*(4), 382–388.

Maguire, M., & Bennett, T. (1982). *Burglary in a dwelling: The offence, the offender, and the victim*. London: Heinemann.

Mawby, R. I. (2001). The impact of repeat victimization on burglary victims in East and West Europe. *Crime Prevention Studies, 12*, 69–82.

Paine, C. (2012). *Solvability factors in dwelling burglaries in Thames Valley* (Unpublished master's thesis).

Robb, P., Coupe, T., & Ariel, B. (2015). "Solvability" and detection of metal theft on railway property. *European Journal on Criminal Policy and Research, 21*(4), 463–484.

6 The future of evidence-based offender profiling

Introduction

Many crimes are unsolved every year, preventing victims from receiving justice and allowing the offenders free to re-offend. Indeed Farrington, Langan, and Tonry (2004) estimated that there were only 7 convictions per 1,000 offenders for burglary, 17 for vehicle theft, 6 for robbery, 25 for serious assault, and 71 for rape in England and Wales in 1999. In the United States in 1996, the conviction rates for 1,000 offenders were 16 for burglary, 13 for vehicle theft, 24 for robbery, 34 for serious assault, and 155 for rape. It is obviously very important to increase the probability that an offender will be caught and convicted for different types of crimes they are committing.

Evidence-based offender profiling (EBOP) has the potential to greatly increase police detection rates. The main aims of EBOP are (1) to classify types of offenses, (2) to classify types of offenders, and (3) to establish statistical regularities between types of offenses and types of offenders so that characteristics of the offender can be predicted from characteristics of unsolved crimes. EBOP can assist the police by narrowing down the range of people who could be offenders. Based on our research, many perpetrators of unsolved crimes are already in police records management systems and databases. EBOP can predict which of these people are most likely to have committed any particular type of unsolved crime. A key issue for future research is the extent to which features of offenders stay constant or change over time; this was investigated in Chapter 3.

This book has traced the development of EBOP from the earliest days of clinical offender profiling. Chapter 2 reviewed some classic cases, including Jack the Ripper, the Yorkshire Ripper, and the Mad Bomber of New York City. According to surveys, clinical profiles were often considered by the police to be useful (e.g., in understanding the offender), but they rarely helped the police to solve cases. Chapter 2 then traced the development of more statistical approaches, including investigative psychology, crime linkage analysis (CLA), and geographic profiling. It also reviewed the use of Behavioral Investigative Advisors (BIAs) by the police.

Chapter 3 described some pioneering research in Nottinghamshire in England in the 1990s that aimed to investigate statistical regularities between types of offenses and types of offenders, for burglary and violence offenses. It was demonstrated that location–site–time–day profiles of offenses and address–age–sex profiles of victims were related to address–age–sex–ethnicity profiles of offenders. How criminals were usually caught were also investigated. Chapter 3 also summarized the main conclusions emerging from a review of the first 40 years of offender profiling research. Over time, studies have become more statistically sophisticated, and recurring profiles have been discovered for homicide, sexual assault, sexual homicide, arson, and burglary. Most research on offender profiling has studied the most serious offenses such as homicide and rape rather than volume crimes such as burglary and vehicle theft. However, there have been very few attempts to evaluate the usefulness of offender profiling in live police investigations.

Chapter 4 described the first development and evaluation of EBOP in Florida, in the United States. Latent class analysis was used to develop profiles of burglary offenses and offenders. The offenses were classified as organized, disorganized, opportunistic, or interpersonal. Organized offenses tended to be committed by older offenders with a long criminal history; disorganized offenses tended to be committed by younger offenders with an early onset of criminal behavior; opportunistic burglars were also young and mainly male, but they included the highest proportion of female burglars; and interpersonal burglars tended to be older and usually knew the victim.

Remarkably, Chapter 4 also described an experimental test of these profiles and statistical regularities in Florida. Detectives in one police department were trained to use these profiles in trying to solve burglaries, while other police departments served as controls. Before the intervention, the burglary arrest rates were comparable in the experimental and control conditions. After the intervention, the burglary arrest rate tripled in the experimental area and decreased slightly in the control areas. This experiment shows the enormous potential of EBOP in assisting police to solve crimes.

Chapter 4 also demonstrated that CLA was remarkably accurate in linking a series of crimes to one offender. This chapter also reviewed research on the development of EBOP profiles of juvenile sex offenders in Florida. Four types of offenders were discovered: non-disordered, impulsive-unempathetic, early-onset chronic, and mentally disordered offenders. These kinds of findings are important not only for police but also for practitioners who seek to understand, treat, and prevent offending.

Chapter 5 described the first development of EBOP profiles in the United Kingdom, again for burglary. Cluster analysis was used to develop profiles of offenses and offenders. Four types of burglaries were identified: Forceful, Skilled-Domestic, Interpersonal, and Non-Domestic. Generally, interpersonal burglaries tended to be committed by adult minority males, Non-Domestic burglaries tended to be committed by young white males, and Skilled-Domestic burglaries tended to be committed by adult white males. Encouragingly, these UK results replicated the Florida findings to some extent. UK Interpersonal offenses were similar to Florida interpersonal offenses, UK Forceful offenses were similar to Florida disorganized offenses, and UK Skilled-Domestic offenses were similar to Florida organized offenses.

These results suggest that the time is ripe to mount a coordinated program of research on EBOP, to develop offense and offender profiles for different types of offenses using sophisticated statistical methods, and to test their usefulness in police investigations experimentally, as in Florida.

Ideally, the police should routinely code and computerize characteristics of offenders, offenses, and victims (not only for the most serious crimes), so that computerized databases and records management systems can be searched to find which types of offenders have committed particular types of offenses in the past to target investigations more efficiently.

We recommend that a small number of police departments in the United Kingdom and United States should implement this data system and experimentally evaluate its usefulness in live investigations. Eventually, BIAs could be trained to use this data and records system to implement EBOP more effectively as a truly scientific method.

Reference

Farrington, D. P., Langan, P. A., & Tonry, M. H. (Eds.). (2004). *Cross-national studies in crime and justice*. Washington, DC: US Department of Justice, Office of Justice Programs, Bureau of Justice Statistics.

Index

For Product Safety Concerns and Information please contact our EU
representative GPSR@taylorandfrancis.com
Taylor & Francis Verlag GmbH, Kaufingerstraße 24, 80331 München, Germany

www.ingramcontent.com/pod-product-compliance
Lightning Source LLC
Chambersburg PA
CBHW050541270326
41926CB00015B/3328